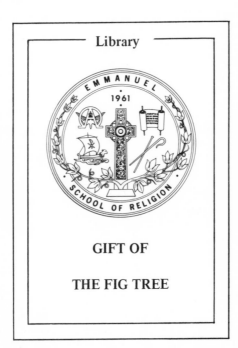

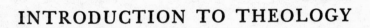

INTRODUCTION TO THEOLOGY

Marianne H. Micks

INTRODUCTION

TO THEOLOGY

A CROSSROAD BOOK
THE SEABURY PRESS • NEW YORK

Fourth Printing

Copyright © 1964 by The Seabury Press, Incorporated

ISBN: 0-8164-2036-X

Library of Congress Catalog Card Number: 64-19622

462-272-C-9-2-5

Printed in the United States of America

First Seabury Paperback *Edition 1967*

ACKNOWLEDGMENTS

The chapters that make up this book have been developed from lectures given at the Orientation Program sponsored by the Division of Christian Ministries for Apprentices in the Episcopal Church in the summer of 1963.

Unless otherwise specified, the biblical quotations are from the Revised Standard Version of the Holy Bible. Frequently, theologians have been cited whose translated works are readily available in paperback editions; specific references will be found in the Notes at the end of the book.

Grateful acknowledgment is made to the following publishers and authors for permission to quote copyrighted material from their publications:

George Braziller, Inc.: from *Judaism,* ed. Arthur Hertzberg.

Cambridge University Press: from *F. D. Maurice and the Conflicts of Modern Theology* by Arthur Michael Ramsey.

Dacre Press: A. & C. Black Ltd.: from *The Glass of Vision* and *A Rebirth of Images* by Austin Farrer.

Doubleday & Company, Inc.: from *Martin Luther,* ed. John Dillenberger. Copyright © 1961 by John Dillenberger. From *The Noise of Solemn Assemblies* by Peter L. Berger. Copyright © 1961 by Peter L. Berger. From *Protestant-Catholic-Jew* by Will Herberg. Copyright © 1960 by Will Herberg. From *Selections from the Writings of Kierkegaard,* tr. Lee M. Hollander. Copyright © 1960 by Lee M. Hollander.

iv

E. P. Dutton & Co. Inc.: from Everyman's Library editions of *The Confessions of St. Augustine,* tr. E. B. Pusey, D. D.; and *Of the Laws of Ecclesiastical Polity* by Richard Hooker.

Farrar, Straus, & Cudahy, Inc.: from *Myth and Christianity* by Karl Jaspers and Rudolf Bultmann.

The Folger Shakespeare Library: from *An Apology of the Church of England* by John Jewel, ed. J. E. Booty. Published by Cornell University Press.

Fortress Press: from *Three Treatises* by Martin Luther.

Harper & Row: from *Dynamics of Faith* by Paul Tillich.

Holt, Rinehart and Winston, Inc.: from *Man for Himself* by Erich Fromm, and from *Peter Abelard* by Helen Waddell.

John Knox Press: from *Anselm: Fides Quaerens Intellectum* by Karl Barth.

The Macmillan Company: from *The Cost of Discipleship* and *Letters and Papers from Prison* by Dietrich Bonhoeffer, and from *The Meaning of Revelation* by H. Richard Niebuhr.

Oxford University Press: from *Christianity and Classical Culture* by Charles Norris Cochrane, and from *Documents of the Christian Church,* ed. Henry Bettenson.

Pacific Churchman: from "Letter to a Bore" by Dorothy L. Sayers.

Random House, Inc.: from *Basic Writings of Saint Augustine,* ed. Whitney J. Oates. Copyright, 1948, by Random House, Inc.

Henry Regnery Company: from *The Letters of St. Bernard of Clairvaux,* tr. Bruno Scott James. Copyright, 1953, by Henry Regnery Company. From *St. Augustine: The Enchiridion on Faith, Hope and Love,* ed. Henry Paolucci, tr. J. F. Shaw. © 1961 by Henry Regnery Company.

Saturday Review: from "The Freedom to Hope" by William Ernest Hocking.

Charles Scribner's Sons: from *Jesus Christ and Mythology* by Rudolf Bultmann, from *Protestant Christianity* by John Dillenberger and Claude Welch, from *The Nature and Destiny of Man* by Reinhold Niebuhr, and from *Reason and Revelation in the Middle Ages* by Etienne Gilson.

The Seabury Press: from *Reinhold Niebuhr: A Prophetic Voice in Our Time,* ed. Harold R. Landon.

Sheed & Ward, Inc.: from *A Monument to St. Augustine,* ed. M. C. D'Arcy.

Simon & Schuster, Inc.: from *The Lonely African* by Colin M. Turnbull. Copyright © 1962 by Colin M. Turnbull.

The Student Christian Movement Press Ltd.: from *Christian Apologetics* by Alan Richardson.

The Viking Press, Inc.: from *Eichmann in Jerusalem* by Hannah Arendt.

A. Watkins, Inc.: from *The Emperor Constantine* by Dorothy L. Sayers. Copyright, 1951 by Dorothy L. Sayers. Published by Victor Gollancz Ltd.

The Westminster Press: from *Augustine: Later Works,* LCC, Vol. VIII, ed. John Burnaby. From *The Bible in the Age of Science* by Alan Richardson. Copyright © 1961, SCM Press, Ltd. From *Christology of the Later Fathers,* LCC, Vol. III, ed. Edward Rochie Hardy. From *Early Christian Fathers,* LCC, Vol. I, ed. Cyril C. Richardson.

TO MARGARET
with thanksgiving

Contents

Introduction

Two convictions have dictated the form and scope of this book. The first is simply that anyone who calls himself a Christian is called upon to think about his faith. The second, that he has inherited resources to help him find joy in the process.

All Christians are under an imperative to be thinking Christians because of the commandment to love the Lord their God with all their hearts, and with all their souls, *and with all their minds*. Whatever intellectual resources one has, whatever benefits of formal education, are to be used in the service of the Lord. Thinking about God or about Christianity is by no means the only thinking which comes under this total claim on one's mental powers, but such thinking is certainly included. I take it that everyone is obliged to use his mind fully and rigorously and persistently in relation to what he calls his religion. Not everyone is called to be a professional theologian, but everyone using the name Christian is called to disciplined thinking about God. Disciplined thinking about God is theology. That very general meaning of the word will be understood throughout these pages.

Put solely in the category of commandment, this sounds like a grim activity. The experience is quite otherwise, because the person who accepts the intellectual dimension of his Christian commitment soon finds that he is part of an exciting community of thinkers. He shares the struggle to find and express a reason for the faith that is in him with some of the greatest minds of all times. And companioned in this way, he knows intellectual adventure. Whether for the first time or only in a new connection, he can glimpse the truth of Whitehead's statement that the final end of education is joy.

The final end, please note. Hard mental effort comes first, in spite of the churches which (in the recent past, at any rate) have condemned their members to religious infantilism by acting as if it were not needed. Many otherwise intelligent Christians are needlessly scared by the word theology. Not having been taught to ventilate their faith with a few healthy doubts, they avoid thinking about it at all, and fall back on the ridiculously un-Christian notion that to have a "simple" faith is a virtue.

Just as ill equipped for an adult faith are the do-it-yourself theologians who see no need for using any of the tools of the trade. Crewel embroidery or electronics call for expertism, but every man can be his own expert in "religion." As often as not this home-grown expert repudiates "theology" along with "dogma" as needless obfuscation. He would not think of reading a book *Plato Without Philosophy* or *Einstein Without Physics,* but he is delighted when someone publishes *The Fathers Without Theology.*[1] Some years ago a lay theologian of distinction, Dorothy Sayers, addressed a stinging letter to such a person, a "Letter to a Bore":

Why, when you can bestir yourselves to "mug up" technical terms about electricity, won't you do as much for theology before you begin to argue about it? Why do you never read either the ancient or modern authorities in the subject . . . why don't you do a hand's turn for yourselves, confound you? You would be ashamed to know as little about internal combustion as you do about the Nicene Creed. I admit that you can practice Christianity without knowing much about theology, just as you can drive a car without understanding internal combustion—but if something breaks down in the car, you go humbly to the man who understands the works, whereas if something goes wrong with your religion you merely throw the creed away and tell the theologian he's a liar.[2]

The situation may be changing in an age which dares be honest to God and to rethink its theology accordingly. Lay theologians as well as professionals are urgently needed for such rethinking. But it cannot be done well if it is done in ignorance of the Christian theological past. And it need not be done in isolation from the contemporary Christian intellectual community.

The resources for the thinking Christian are threefold. In classical terms, there are three authorities in theology—scripture, tradition, and reason. The proper mode of combining these sources is a matter of debate among the several branches of the Christian family, each with a different recipe for mixing the ingredients. Hence there is an acknowledged problem of authority in Christian thinking, an old problem currently receiving fresh attention as a result of the ecumenical movement. Fortunately, no theologian needs to settle the problem before he begins to think about God. On the contrary, since he needs all the help he can get to think about this problem along with the others, he does well to explore all sorts of theological writing.

Accordingly, this book has been divided into three parts, roughly parallel to the three sources of authority. The first seeks to introduce the field of biblical theology, in order to help the reader use scripture intelligently in his own thinking. The second deals with historical theology, not to define the role of tradition, but to present something of the part it plays in Christian thought. In the third, some recent and contemporary theologians are spokesmen for the apologetic task of communicating the Christian gospel in a world that respects reason more readily than it respects either scripture or tradition. Patently, no attempt can be made to present the fulness of the Christian theological inheritance in this brief compass. Nor to offer either new or fixed answers to theological questions. The intent is rather to mark more clearly all three major entrances into the large spaces of Christian thought, to describe the basic tools for the part-time theologian entering these doors, and to introduce some of his co-workers in the job of learning to love the Lord his God with all his mind.

PART I

THINKING WITH THE BIBLE

CHAPTER 1

Remembered
History

When anyone in the Western world begins to think about God, he is dependent on the Bible. His fundamental presuppositions about the word *God* are forever colored by biblical thought. His intellectual heritage for two thousand years is imbued with its ideas. Quotation from it and allusion to it fill his literature. He may be unaware of the influence it has on his thinking. Consciously he may reject the authority of scripture completely. But if he reads and thinks at all, it is impossible for him to escape from the Bible.

THE INFLUENCE OF THE BIBLE

The Christian acknowledges the Bible as an indispensable source for disciplined thinking about God. All Christian theology is ultimately linked with the Bible, for the Bible contains the record of God's revelation to man in

3

Jesus Christ. Christians differ greatly, of course, in their emphasis on the Bible as a basis for theology. Some descendants of the Protestant Reformers still take *sola scriptura* as a watchword; some descendants of the Council of Trent still argue for the truth contained *both* in written books *and* in unwritten traditions. Both are guilty of oversimplifying their ancestors; and in this age of ecumenical interest, theologians are engaged in a new effort to express with precision just what weight is to be given to the written word. How that written word is to be interpreted remains a perennial problem in all Christian thinking.

Whatever the method of interpreting scripture, however, or whatever the refinements in expressing its authority, Christians agree that the Bible is the foundation of Christian theology. This is no less true for the Roman Catholic than for the Fundamentalist. Although different words would be used today, the sixteenth-century definition still expresses the substance of mainstream Protestant thinking on the subject:

Holy Scripture containeth all things necessary to salvation: so that whatsoever is not read therein, nor may be proved thereby, is not to be required of any man, that it should be believed as an article of the Faith, or be thought requisite or necessary to salvation.[1]

If the influence of the Bible is thus inescapable and if the authority of the Bible for Christians is thus axiomatic, how should I use it in my thinking about reality? I may consider the Bible a great monument of English literature and turn occasionally to the cadence of the King James Version as an antidote for too much banal writing. Or I may prefer a modern translation from which I can extract lofty ethical concepts, ignoring parts about an anthropomorphic God long outgrown. I may even accept the label *Holy Scripture* and so leave a black, limp-leather edition on my bedside table, where it has been gathering dust since I gave up trying to wade through the "begats" of Genesis. Believing it to be the Word of God, I may open it at random in times of crisis, to seek spiritual uplift or miraculous solutions to personal problems.

Obviously none of these familiar attitudes toward the Bible, caricatured or not, does justice to the claim that this book is the basis of Christian thinking. None of the catchwords is adequate for the intelligent person who asks what the Bible has to tell him about God and man and their relationship. Valid answers to this question depend upon the answer to a prior question. Before one can rightly use the Bible in his theology, he must first decide what the Bible is.

What is the Bible? The Bible is a historical document. More accurately, it is an anthology or collection of historical documents, an ancient book which assumed its present form about the middle of the second century. To say that the Bible is a historical document in this sense is to insist that the Bible has a history. The detailed study of this history provides a lifetime of work and fascination for biblical scholars who follow the disciplines of textual criticism, literary criticism, or form criticism. Their conclusions cannot be ignored by the theologians. They raise basic questions for any Christian thinker who takes seriously the statement that the Bible has a history.

Over a period of centuries, many different men, living in various parts of the ancient Near Eastern and Mediterranean worlds, produced the writings ultimately collected and canonized as Holy Scripture. The oldest written document of any length probably dates from around 1150 B.C., the latest from around A.D. 150. The intellectual differences between the author of the Song of Deborah in the Book of Judges and the author of the Second Epistle of Peter are easily as great as those between William the Conqueror and Astronaut Cooper, or between Chaucer and Camus. How can their contributions to an anthology be thought to express equally valid ideas about God?

All, or almost all, of the so-called authors of these sixty-six documents, furthermore, were themselves drawing on earlier oral traditions. Some of the traditions stretch back to the remote past of the ancient Israelites, to the very dawn of history. How did a historian in the court of King David or King Solomon know what had happened to his ancestors in Ur or in Egypt hundreds of years before? No one tape-recorded the speeches of Jesus. How can the gospel-writer a full generation after his death be so certain of what he said?

In addition to the long and complicated pre-history of the biblical writings, there is an equally long and complicated post-history to be acknowledged and explored. Since the imaginary day when the completed collection left the desk of its final editor, it has been copied and recopied by hand countless times; it has been translated and retranslated in whole or in part into more than 1,100 languages and dialects. Anyone reading the letters to Corinth in the New English Bible, for example, must of necessity wonder what resemblance the Greek manuscript used by the translators bears to the words Paul dictated to his secretary. Certainly he must ask whether this contemporary English idiom means to him anything like what the original letters meant to the congregation of first-century Christians in that bustling commercial center of the Roman Empire.

This further dimension of difficulty, the problem of communication involved in translation, is sharply illustrated by an anthropologist's recent comment on the opening lines of the Fourth Gospel. An African listening to them in his own tribal dialect, we are told, because of his own experience and his experience of European usage of his language, would most likely understand the following: "In the beginning there was a great argument, and the argument came with God, and the argument entered into God." The full seriousness of the problem is underlined when he adds, "And judging by the multitude of missionaries and sects and their differences of opinion, this is not an unreasonable interpretation of God." [2]

THE BIBLE AS HISTORY

Recognition that the Bible has a history involves the thinking Christian in all these questions. There is another, and theologically a more important, level of meaning in the statement that the Bible is a historical document, however. It not only has a history; it *is* history. Centrally, fundamentally, the Bible is about history. From beginning to end, these writings are about things that happened to men and women, living and loving and fighting and dying. It deals with a group of nomadic tribes infiltrating previously settled agricultural lands in a small segment of the Fertile Crescent. It deals with their struggles to become a nation. It tells primarily of their losing battle for survival as a nation—of international intrigue, of wars and rumors of war, of invasion and deportation and rebellion. A struggle which is climaxed when Roman occupation troops execute the man who is a potential threat to Rome's uneasy hold over part of her Syrian province.

As history, the Bible is every bit as much concerned with politics and economics as with what we call religion. How can writings about the national and international affairs of Egypt, Assyria, Babylonia, Persia, Rome, and Palestine be important for my thinking about God? Why should these events of the past have any more significance for an American in the second half of the twentieth century than the political tensions and upheavals of the Middle East headlined in the morning newspaper? With these questions, arising from the uncompromisingly historical quality of the biblical writings, we have come to the heart of the matter. Christians believe that the Bible is an authoritative source for knowledge of ultimate reality. On first inspection by an honest inquirer, it looks to be a very unpromising source indeed. At no point does it offer anything like a proof for the existence of God or a reasoned discourse on his nature and attributes. Neither the Hebrew people nor their heirs, the early Christians, were philosophers. They did not engage in speculative thought. Nor do they offer a systematic, orderly presentation of basic Christian doctrine or of basic Christian ethics. Instead, they offer history.

Biblical history shares with other history, therefore, two characteristics which affect its use in our thinking about the meaning of life. When we turn to these historical documents as a theological source, we must expect, in the first place, to find an interpretation of events. Secondly, this interpretation has been remembered and handed down within a particular community.

First, the Bible offers an interpretation of historical events. All historical writing ends up being interpretative, of course. There is no such thing as objective history in the sense of uninterpreted events. Consider the rear-end collision you were involved in on the way to the grocery store. What happened? As the driver of the first car, stopped for the red light, you will have one version of the incident. The driver of the second car will have another. You did not even see the child who distracted him by running off the curb after a ball. The pedestrian waiting to cross the street, the policeman who takes the report, the insurance adjustor whose lunch is interrupted by your phone call—which one will have the most adequate interpretation of this event?

On a wider screen, look at two accounts of a decisive moment in our national past:

On July 4, 1776, Congress passed the resolution which made the colonies independent communities, issuing at the same time the well-known Declaration of Independence. If we regard the Declaration as the assertion of an abstract political theory, criticism and condemnation are easy. It sets out with a general proposition so vague as to be practically useless. The doctrine of the equality of men, unless it be qualified and conditioned by reference to special circumstance, is either a barren truism or a delusion.

Or, in more familiar words:

Fourscore and seven years ago our fathers brought forth on this continent a new nation, conceived in liberty and dedicated to the proposition that all men are created equal.

Both are unquestionably interpretative. The issue is whether the historian writing for *The Cambridge Modern History* or the President at Gettysburg interprets that Fourth of July more adequately.[3]

The distinctive thing about the biblical account of history is that it views events in relation to the will and purpose and activity of God. It interprets them theologically. For the biblical writers, the ordinary and extraordinary movements of human affairs—the comings and goings of people, the rise and fall of governments—are significant because they are seen as the means by which God makes himself known to men. A single German word is frequently used to express this characteristic bias of the Bible. Biblical history is *heilsgeschichte*, sacred history. The compound word underlines the fact that biblical theology is not, and cannot be, divorced from biblical history. Ask the Bible about God; it will tell you what God did in human society, in the lives of particular men and women. It will not tell you about God apart from the concrete events, because God is known to the people of biblical faith only in this way. As contemporary scholarship continually insists, the Bible is the book of the mighty acts of God.[4]

When the peculiar nature of the biblical record is expressed in this way, however, it is necessary to remember that these events were not self-evidently the acts of God. There was no compelling necessity to interpret them in this way.

Your story of the smashed bumper on your car was not the only possible story. Abraham Lincoln's evaluation of the Declaration of Independence was not the only possible evaluation. In the same way, the Egyptians who presumably heard about the escape of some Israelite slaves in the second millennium B.C. found other, to them perfectly reasonable, interpretations of this minor border incident. Dozens of people, Romans and Jews, watched the crucifixion of Jesus without saying, "Surely this man was the Son of God."

Biblical theology rests on the coalescence of event and interpretation. There is no thought of God in the Bible apart from the evidence of what he has done in history. Equally, there is no biblical record of history apart from the conviction that God was active in it. Every area of human life is interpreted from a theological perspective. The God who speaks through the Bible is by nature one who takes part in the everyday affairs of men. To interpret affairs in this way is a response of faith.

The *second* characteristic of biblical history which responsible theologians must take into account is that it is written in the mood of the first person plural. These are communal documents. The events of which the Bible speaks are not only interpreted; they are remembered within a community. The people of God, the Church, could well be defined as the community that remembers. The Bible offers a family history.

Every lay psychologist is familiar, from television or tabloid, with stories of a man who has forgotten who he is. The man has had a traumatic experience or a blow on the head of sufficient force to make him forget his past history. He is suffering from amnesia. The victim of amnesia—and we tend to use that phrase—no longer knows who he is because he cannot remember what has happened to him. His identity depends on his personal history. Without the knowledge of that unique series of individual experiences which have made him who he is, he is a sick man.

It is instructive to follow an etymological clue here. The word *amnesia* is the first cousin of the Greek term used by liturgical scholars for the distinctive act of Christian worship. Jesus instructed his disciples to do something in remembrance of him. His instructions are obeyed explicitly at every celebration of the Holy Communion. That age-old part of the eucharistic prayer, at which the worshiping community offers bread and wine with a solemn memorial of all that Christ has done through his death, resurrection, and ascension, is known as the *Anamnesis*, the not-forgetting. The terminology is appropriate to the nature of the Christian Church. It rightly suggests that this community is what it is, is who it is, through remembering its own unique past.

Influenced by modern individualism, many Christians find it hard to think that what happened to Jesus affects them in any direct, intelligible way. It is even harder for Christians to accept the theory that what happened to a small group of semi-nomads in the Sinai Peninsula, some three thousand years ago and more, makes them who they are. But this is a fundamental premise of biblical thought. If the Bible is to have a significant impact on anyone's thinking, the history it remembers must be entered into as one's own history.

When second-graders in Iowa or Hawaii make black paper hats each November and re-enact the First Thanksgiving, they are not all blood descendants of the men who first stepped on Plymouth Rock. But the Pilgrim fathers of their celebration are their forefathers nonetheless. When Abraham Lincoln declared that our fathers brought forth upon this continent a new nation, he was not speaking only to those whose blood ancestors signed the Declaration of Independence. He was inviting his listeners to the deliberate act of standing inside the history which he recalled. His words are addressed then and now to all Americans, including the most recent immigrants from Ireland or Poland or China. To choose to be an American, to say this "our," meant and means to choose this history as one's own.

What is true for American history is true also for biblical history. In its manner of speaking in the first person plural, the Old Testament contains a striking parallel to the Gettysburg Address:

When your son asks you in time to come, "What is the meaning of the testimonies and the statutes and the ordinances which the Lord our God has commanded you?" then you shall say to your son, "We were Pharaoh's slaves in Egypt; and the Lord brought us out of Egypt with a mighty hand; and the Lord showed signs and wonders, great and grievous, against Egypt and against Pharaoh and all his household, before our eyes; and he brought us out from there, that he might bring us in and give us the land which he swore to give to our fathers" (*Deut. 6:20-23*).

This passage from Deuteronomy contains the essence of the Passover Haggadah, the liturgy for the annual remembering of Israel's past history on the great feast day. Jewish tradition emphasizes and elaborates what it means to say: "*We* were Pharaoh's slaves in Egypt." At the Seder meal, after the story of the Exodus is recited in response to the youngest son's questions about the meaning of the service, the father explains further:

If the Holy One, praised be He, had not brought our forefathers out of Egypt, then we, our children and our children's children, would be slaves to Pharaoh in Egypt. . . . In every generation a person is obliged to see himself as though he personally came out of Egypt, as it is written: "This is because of what the Lord did for me when I left Egypt." It was not our ancestors alone that the Holy One, praised be He, redeemed. But He redeemed us as well, along with them. . . . He brought us out of slavery into freedom, out of sorrow into happiness, out of mourning into a holiday. . . .[5]

Biblical history, then, has meaning today to men and women who have made this history their own internal history and who call the events into the present through remembering, to participate in their meaning and power. Beyond this, it can be argued that the Bible originally came into being and continues to exist today only because men and women through the ages thus remembered in the context of worship. As dozens of passages in both the Old Testament and the New testify, the occasion of community worship was the structured occasion for remembering.

The Passover was only one such high point in the annual Hebrew calendar. A similar recital, reviewing the past, recalling it to the present, is preserved, for example, in Deuteronomy 26:5-10, a temple liturgy for the feast of the Presentation of First Fruits. The Psalms, the hymnbook of the temple, include many such condensations of the nation's history, to be sung as an integral part of regular worship. One version of the Ten Commandments, indeed, suggests that the Sabbath itself was instituted to provide an occasion for historical memory:

The seventh day is a sabbath to the Lord your God; in it you shall not do any work. . . . You shall remember that you were a servant in the land of Egypt, and the Lord your God brought you out thence with a mighty hand and an outstretched arm; therefore the Lord your God commanded you to keep the sabbath day (*Deut. 5:14-15*).

As people came to write down the memories recited in worship and to expand them, the writings in turn were cherished and preserved by the community, to be read aloud when they gathered to worship. The role of the cult in producing and preserving the historical documents of the Bible is not yet fully explored; some scholars find that it is in danger of being exaggerated into a single causal factor. Were it not for the cult, however, almost certainly there would have been no scrolls of sacred history, nor such devoted efforts to keep them safe from the enemy. The library of Qumrân, discovered in caves near the Dead Sea, is only one testimony to the part played by the worshiping community in handing down the Bible to the twentieth century.

THE LANGUAGE OF REMEMBERING

Just as biblical archeologists and historians are indebted to worshipers, so too are biblical theologians. Recognizing the decisive role of the cult in the formation of the Bible has for them a further implication, one which sharply affects their efforts to think the thoughts of the biblical writers. The cult contributed not only the occasion for remembering but also the language of remembering. Much of the language of the Bible is the language appropriate to worship. This means, on the one hand, that it is the language of story, of narrative. It means, on the other hand, that it is personal language, the language of relationship. The language in which the events of the past are interpreted and remembered is an integral part of the interpreting and remembering. Form and content are so interdependent that one cannot change the one without grave violence to the other.

Searching questions have been raised in our day, and must be raised, about the possibility and necessity of changing the language of biblical thought. The issue is one to which we must return, in order to explore it at greater length and depth. As one enters the realm of biblical thought, however, the effort must first be to hear it in its own tongue. Only after that effort has been made can one come to speak in other tongues the wonderful works of God as the Bible understands them.

What the Bible has to say to Christian thinking about God and man, we have seen, is to be found in a historical document sharing many characteristics of other historical documents. It is concerned throughout with historical events interpreted as the acts of God through the lives of human beings, events remembered by the community in the context and language of worship. The major acts are quite specific and concrete. The theological implications of the Bible must be drawn from them or not at all.

CHAPTER 2

From Exodus
to Creation

Sometime in the thirteenth century B.C. a group of Hebrew people who had been in forced labor in Egypt managed to escape. This is what the people of Israel remembered every Sabbath as well as on the major feast days. This is the pivot on which the whole Old Testament and much of the New swings. This is the basic experience which told the Israelites what ultimate reality is like.

EXODUS: THE BIBLICAL EVENT

The importance of the Exodus from Egypt in determining biblical thought can hardly be overemphasized. The story has been greatly elaborated within the scriptures and without. Although men have spent years in devoted, skilled research trying to establish when and how it actually happened, the sure results are minimal. The oppression can be dated with a high degree of probability in the reign of Pharaoh Rameses

II (1290-1223 B.C.), whose building program included the two store cities mentioned in Exodus 1:11. The cities were in the delta region of the Nile; and so, with the same high degree of probability, the point of departure from Egypt can be placed near the modern Suez Canal. That the Red Sea crossing of tradition rests on an ancient mistranslation of "reed sea" is a long-known and well-known conclusion of biblical study, even if many people still prefer to picture a technicolored Exodus according to Hollywood.

In the eyes of the Israelites who remembered the event, the geography of the escape route was apparently secondary. So were the details of what happened to the pursuing detachment of Egyptian soldiers. One very ancient description of their downfall merely records the essentials in a tantalizing couplet:

Sing to the Lord, for he has triumphed gloriously; the horse and his rider he has thrown into the sea (*Ex. 15:21*).

The importance of the occurrence rests, not on the how, but on the what:

We were Pharaoh's slaves in Egypt; and the Lord brought us out of Egypt with a mighty hand.

To this central historical memory of the Exodus, two other events have been added as prologue and epilogue in Israel's sacred history, so that the past comes in three acts. Long before the Exodus, God had made a promise to the patriarch Abraham, when he still lived beyond the Euphrates River. After the Exodus, God fulfilled the promise by bringing Abraham's descendants safely into the land of Israel. In their completed form, the first six books of the Bible, the Hexateuch, are a dramatic telling of this threefold story. The rest of the Old Testament is an extended commentary on its implications. Why? What did this mean to Israel?

The Bible, let us repeat, gives the answer only in the language of narrative. Three different examples of the re-telling of the tale will help us approach its theological implications. The first is found in the final chapter of the Hexateuch, chapter 24 of the book of Joshua. Joshua, the military commander of the Israelite forces, has summoned the leaders of all the tribes to Shechem, an ancient holy place, for a ceremony of covenant renewal before God. Israel has not yet become a monarchy; the tribes are tied together, somewhat loosely it seems, by common allegiance to the Lord, Yahweh, and for common defense of shrines devoted to his name. But already the bonds of this confederation are weakened by the attractions to other deities. To the newcomers in this land, the religion of the Canaanite people among whom they lived seemed both more sophisticated and more relevant.

In this situation, as the story now stands, Joshua counters the threat to political and religious unity by reminding his leaders of their past experience. In the name of Yahweh, God of Israel, he reviews the sacred history: "I took your father Abraham from beyond the River. . . . Then I brought your fathers out of Egypt. . . . I gave you a land on which you had not labored and cities which you had not built, and you dwell therein. . . . Now therefore fear the Lord." Other details of the history are included, but the essential outline is clear. The "therefore" is the point of the recital. Because of this three-act past, Joshua calls for decision in the present: "Choose this day whom you will serve . . . but as for me and my house, we will serve the Lord." The priority of the Exodus is indicated afresh as the people respond, "Far be it from us that we should foresake the Lord, to serve other gods; for it is Yahweh our God who brought us and our fathers up from the land of Egypt, out of the house of bondage."

Similar summaries of the basic events recur in Psalms

105 and 106. Taken as a complementary pair, they contain the same interpreted facts as the call for covenant renewal in Joshua. In Psalm 105, composed for festival worship, the congregation is invited to sing of the mighty works of Yahweh, to tell of his deeds: He made a covenant with Abraham, promising the land. Abraham's descendants became enslaved in Egypt, but Yahweh led them forth. He gave them the lands of the nations. The power of this song of praise lies in the cumulative force of the active verbs used of God: he summoned, he sent, he turned, he spoke, he gave, he led, he smote, he opened—he remembered.

Psalm 106 uses the Exodus story as a backdrop, focusing on the incongruous behavior of the people who had been rescued. God's action in history is contrasted with the Israelites' response in history. Again, it is the verbs which demand attention, but the stress is now on the verbs used of the people. Concrete, specific incidents are recalled to prove that, from the time of their deliverance from Egypt to their present dispersion among the nations (at least seven hundred years later), they have sinned, rebelled, murmured, mingled, provoked. And, most emphatically, they have forgotten.

These three selections from the Old Testament present fundamental themes of biblical faith in typical fashion. What God is like is known through what he does. What man is like is known through his response. Doctrines about God and man are necessarily abstractions from this story of Abraham and Egypt and the Promised Land. Generalization and abstraction are uncharacteristic of the Hebrew mind, but for the modern Western mind they are an integral part of the intellectual process. This difference must be recognized in order to try to correct, in so far as possible, the distortion it may lead to in summarizing biblical thought. To be valid, what is abstracted should truly be present in and important to the narrated events.

THEOLOGICAL INTERPRETATIONS

What theological conclusions may one legitimately draw from these examples of the concrete memories of Israel? The three-act drama seems to demand three principal conclusions; and if it is true that the second act, the Exodus, comes first in importance, then the conclusion from this experience rightly heads the list. First and foremost, what the Bible says about God, when it says nothing else, is that God frees people. He is the source, and his is the power, of freedom. At the beginning of the Decalogue, God is self-identified as, and only as, the one who rescues the oppressed: "I am the Lord your God who brought you out of the land of Egypt, out of the house of bondage. You shall have no other gods before me" (*Ex. 20:2;* cf. *Deut. 5:6*).

In the Revised Standard Version, the liturgical passages cited earlier from Deuteronomy express this idea by repeating the phrase, God "brought us out from there." The new Jewish translation of the Torah[1] chooses instead the single, unequivocal English word *freed:* "The Lord your God freed you from there" (*Deut. 5:15, 6:23, 26:8*). The 106th psalm makes the same point by giving God the title *Saviour.* It declares not only that "he saved them from the hand of the foe and delivered them from the power of the enemy," but also that "many times he delivered them." What was found to be true of God through the experience of coming out of Egypt became the interpretative key to other, later experiences of the Israelite people. When, for example, the poet Second Isaiah yearns for the deliverance of his people from exile in Babylon, centuries later, he is confident that there will be a second Exodus (e.g., *Isa. 43:14ff.*). And he uses the still more familiar title *Redeemer* to convey this same essential quality of Israel's God.

The second aspect of divine activity emphasized by the

biblical drama is closely related to the first. The God who gives freedom is also one who chooses freely. The biblical doctrine of election results from this choosing characteristic of God. He has chosen for himself a people, a choice represented by Abraham, the patriarch to whom he promised the land for his offspring. The idea of the chosen people causes much confusion in the minds of some Christians. It seems so undemocratic, they say, for God to play favorites. When one remembers the degree to which election is part of democratic action as we understand it, this seems a curious complaint to make; but the reason for it is understandable enough. We should like to have God conform to our unrealized standards of impartiality.

Some of Israel's thinkers were equally puzzled when they tried to explain why God had chosen them. They knew most clearly what did *not* explain it. It was not, for example, because of their great numbers (*Deut. 7:7*), and it was surely not because of their outstanding righteousness (*Deut. 9:6*). Instead of trying to analyze divine motives, the psalmist we have been listening to merely calls upon the offspring of Abraham, "his chosen ones," to sing of the inexplicable wonders of what God did when they were few in number and of little account (*Ps. 105:12*). Here again, God's action implies his nature. He is himself unconditioned. He chooses unconditionally.

The third in the trilogy of events at the core of Israel's remembered history emphasizes yet a third major characteristic of this active God. He who brought the people into the land had thereby demonstrated that he remembers his promises and fulfills them. Although he cannot be judged by human standards, although he is in no way dependent on men, he is faithful rather than fickle. He can be counted on. According to the psalmist, his trustworthiness is unlimited: "He is mindful of his covenant for ever, of the word that he commanded for a thousand generations" (*Ps. 105:8*).

Psalm 106 talks about this when it speaks of "the abundance of his steadfast love." *Steadfast love* (RSV) expresses
the single Hebrew word *chesed,* usually translated *mercy*
in the King James Version. According to studies such as
that of Norman Snaith in *A Theological Word Book of the
Bible,* the word was widely used in connection with all cove-
nants, human as well as divine.[2] It is very close in meaning to
loyalty. *Chesed* is the personal characteristic of the reliable
God as Israel knew him through its history. It is also the attitude appropriate to both parties of a covenant relationship.

The earliest Old Testament writers did not make much
use of the more general Hebrew word for love when speaking
of God's attitude toward man; but the eighth-century prophet
Hosea, as well as later writers, employed it freely. Hosea pictures God's relationship to his covenant people in vivid
metaphors of human experience. God is the husband of a
harlot wife he cannot give up; he is the parent of a rebellious
child he cannot disown. In one of the most moving bits of
poetry in the whole Bible, we hear once more from Hosea
how deeply convictions about God's nature are rooted in
Israel's past:

> When Israel was a child, I loved him,
>   and out of Egypt I called my son.
> The more I called them,
>   the more they went from me. . . .
> Yet it was I who taught Ephraim to walk,
> I took them up in my arms;
>   but they did not know that I healed them.
> I led them with cords of compassion,
>   with the bands of love. . . .
> How can I give you up, O Ephraim!
> How can I hand you over, O Israel!
>   (*Hos. 11:1-4a,8*).

The central biblical doctrines of redemption, election,
and covenant therefore stem from a particular historical ex-

perience. The Bible's peculiar emphasis on this history makes
biblical thought decisively different from the thought of
other ancient peoples. Two of these differences are greatly
emphasized, and rightly so, in contemporary biblical theology. In biblical faith, time matters. So does personal decision. In contrast to the thought of the Babylonians or the
Assyrians or the Egyptians or the Canaanites—as well as in
contrast to the Greeks—Hebrew thought is dynamic. The
Hebrew people had a past which was different from their
present; they looked forward to a still different future. History is not cyclical, endlessly repeating itself. Real changes
occur. And consequently human choices matter too. As God
has chosen a people and remembered them, so man is called
upon to choose and serve God. There is room for personal
responsibility in the biblical view of life, as there is not in
the world views of the other peoples in the ancient Near East.[3]
So it is with urgency that a Joshua presses his leaders to choose
this day whom they will serve (*Josh. 24:15*). That an Elijah
taunts the people for limping eternally between two opinions, unable to make up their minds which god to worship
(*I Kings 18:21*).

Nevertheless, the biblical concern for history can be
overemphasized. In its defense of the uniqueness of the biblical God, much current interpretation seems in danger of
denying its own premise—that God works through history.
Precisely because he does work in this way, the Bible insists
that he works through nature too. The Israelites neither
lived nor thought in a cultural vacuum. They were in constant contact through the centuries with the developed civilizations of Egypt and Mesopotamia. When they settled down
in the Promised Land, they lived literally next door to Canaanite nature religion. As the story of Joshua 24 indicates,
along with dozens of others, they always faced the temptation
to be just like other nations. They frequently succumbed to
it. There is no doubt whatsoever that the intercultural re-

lationships of the tribes of Israel affected their whole way of life, including their theology.

In the thousand years between the Exodus and the time of the Maccabees, when the Book of Daniel was written, thinking about God developed and changed. This was by no means a straight-line growth, onward and upward, such as nineteenth-century ideas of evolution drew for biblical thought. The older historians of religion imported a false suggestion of progress—as if the poor, simple nomads of the desert gradually outgrew their narrow little tribal god and reasoned their way to an arithmetical One. At the end point of this process of enlightenment, they used to submit as Exhibit A the ideas of "monotheism" and "universalism" which they found in the sixth-century prophet Second Isaiah. The evidence suggests rather that the events of history led later Israelites to make explicit what was already implicit in their interpreted experience. Whatever the timing of this development, the Bible in its final form declares from the beginning that Yahweh the God of history is also the God of nature, and that Yahweh the God of Israel is also the God of all people. The doctrine of creation, including the creation of man, is part of the oldest stratum of the Pentateuch.

THE CONCEPT OF DIVINE KINGSHIP

From the standpoint of biblical theology, the more important change in Israel's life and thought resulting from cultural contact with other nations was political: Israel chose a king. The tribal confederation of Joshua's day was replaced by a monarchy. The hindsight of later generations (which had experienced the king's taxes) wants to give the impression that religious leaders resisted the change at the time. One account of choosing Saul as the first king for the united nation insists that the prophet Samuel was extremely reluctant to anoint a monarch, knowing even then that it meant a rejection of the direct sovereignty of God. According to I Samuel 8:7, the Lord said to Samuel at the time, ". . . they have rejected me from being king over them."

What it means to think of God as king was evidently a matter of theological debate in ancient Israel. It is also a matter of scholarly debate in the twentieth century, particularly in relation to the idea of kingship reflected in the psalms. But because Israel acquired a king, and because it had contact with other monarchies, a kingship metaphor plays an important role in biblical theology. The language of kingship forbids exaggerated separation of history from nature in biblical interpretation.

The king was a religious figure in all of the ancient Near East. In theory and in practice, he played a dual role. On the one hand, he was a representative of his people before the gods. He embodied in his person, as it were, the whole community, the whole social organism. At the same time, he was also conceived of as a representative of the gods to his people. In this capacity the king took a leading part in the dramatic re-enactments of the myths which expressed the people's understanding of reality. Their re-enactment assured the ordered continuance of this reality. Thus in the creation myth of the Babylonians, for example, chaos is overcome when one of the gods slays the monster of the deep. The annual festival in which the king engaged in mimetic combat with this dragon was a symbolic representation of the battle between order and chaos, life and death, summer and winter, old year and new. The ritual ended with a triumphant procession of the divine victor in the symbolic person of the king, followed by his solemn enthronement to rule over the people for another year.

Such a condensed summary of the complex idea of kingship in the ancient world does justice neither to the intellectual achievement of ancient man nor to that of modern scholarship in reconstructing this world of myth and ritual.[4] But it will serve to suggest the kind of thinking about kings with which the Israelites undoubtedly had direct contact, and which undoubtedly left its mark on biblical thought about God as king. The contemporary debate concerns only the amount of influence it had—raising such questions as whether Israel itself had an annual enthronement festival for the new year. About the fact of influence, there is no question.

For our purposes, the important point to emphasize from this excursus is that monarchy and nature were inextricably interwoven in the thought of agricultural peoples. When the Hebrew people became agriculturalists and took to themselves a king, they related the idea of divine kingship to Yahweh, God of Israel. For biblical faith, the prior fact about God was and remained his rule of history; but the metaphor of kingship implied also his rule of the natural order. Biblical thinking begins with salvation and extends to creation.

These broad dimensions of kingship theology are most evident in the psalms. Psalm 95, for example, the basis of the *Venite* at the opening of the Anglican Order of Morning Prayer, makes it eminently clear that the Lord, the strength (or rock) of our salvation, is also maker and ruler of all the corners of the earth. The mountains and the sea are in *his* hands:

> For the Lord is a great God
> and a great King above all gods.

This psalm is one of a group of kingship psalms, celebrating the reign of the Lord. Each of them, from 95 to 99, has been associated with the disputed enthronement festival; in each of them both history and nature are invoked as witnesses to the divine sovereignty. Although they do not use the kingship language explicitly, the praise and thanksgiving of Psalms 135 and 136 celebrate notably the same combination of salvation and creation. He who smote the firstborn of Egypt to free his people is he who makes lightnings for the rain. The sun which he made to rule over the day and the overthrow of Pharaoh's host are equal evidence of his steadfast love which endures forever. He who remembered and rescued Israel "gives food to all flesh, for his steadfast love endures for ever" (*Ps. 136:25*).

The psalms are not alone in supplying examples of how the idea of divine kingship was historicized in biblical thought and used to express God's omnipotence and universalism. The prophet Isaiah also thought in memorable terms of God as king. Isaiah's vision in the Temple, described in chapter 6, occurred—be it noted—in the year that the old king Uzziah had died and a new one was anointed. Some commentators see the imagery, therefore, in the light of the enthronement ceremony which Israel might well have used to install a new monarch in office. Whether or not Isaiah was actually watching a coronation, he certainly thought of God in pictures of kingship. One look at the winged creatures carved on the royal thrones of antiquity[5] is enough to suggest their connection with the seraphim surrounding the Lord, high and lifted up, with his train filling the temple—even without the soul-shaken declaration, "My eyes have seen the King, the Lord of hosts!" (*Isa. 6:5*).

The prophet knows assuredly in his vision that the Lord is king of the whole earth. But this justly familiar chapter of the Old Testament adds two further facets to the idea of divine kingship as it was naturalized in biblical theology. The vision is granted to Isaiah, first, at a moment of national crisis. With the Assyrians already on the horizon, threatening the continued independence of the little states which stood be-

tween her and her imperial dreams, he was understandably
worried about what a change in human kingship might mean
for national security. Although the vision implies the creation of nature when it calls God a king, by no stretch of the
imagination can this creator be thought of as the watchmaker
of deism, who made the world and left it to tick on by itself.
The reign of this king is an active reign, in the present—the
reign of one prepared to name an ambassador to take part in
foreign-policy decisions of the little nation state. The whole
earth is full of his glory, but he says to Isaiah, "Go, and say
to this people. . . ."

In the experience of Isaiah, secondly, as in the experience
of ancient peoples generally, a king by definition was also a
judge. Hence the kingship psalms we have referred to call
him judge as well as ruler, in almost automatic parallelism.
For Isaiah, the encounter with transcendent holiness which
he describes by saying he has seen the King, meant also an
encounter with judgment. He is conscious that he is a man
of unclean lips, dwelling among a people of unclean lips. But
the judge whom Isaiah meets in this moment in the temple
is the judge who says, "Your guilt is taken away and your sin
forgiven" (Isa. 6:7).

We have said that as men of biblical faith learned to
think of God as king, they thought of him as creator and
judge as well as Saviour. We have also said that biblical
thinkers took time seriously, that there is a real past and
present and future in biblical thought. As the idea of kingship helped to extend the idea of God's sovereignty back to
the beginning, to the creation of all things, so too the idea of
kingship helped to shape biblical ideas of the future. The
hope of Israel was expressed in terms of the future establish-
ment of God's kingdom. And the concrete, historical character of biblical thought gave color and detail to that future
kingdom. It would be ruled over by the true King's repre-

sentative, his anointed one, his Messiah. Under the influence of kingship ideas encountered in its history, but with an all-important difference born of its own distinctive theology, Israel came to look for another king of the line of David.

CHAPTER 3

From Resurrection
to Incarnation

In the reign of Tiberius Caesar, Pontius Pilate being governor of Judea, Jesus of Nazareth was crucified. According to the Gospel narratives, he had had a short public career. He had preached about the kingdom of God in his home province of Galilee. Accompanied by some friends, he had traveled in adjoining territories which were also under Roman rule. At the time of the annual festival in commemoration of the Exodus, he had gone up to the Jewish capital to participate in the celebration there. In the midst of the holiday excitement, he was arrested, tried, and executed. On the third day he rose again.

THE NEW TESTAMENT EVENT

Our twentieth century has rediscovered the Old Testament. It has also rediscovered thereby the great unity of the

Bible, the tremendous continuity between the Old Testament and the New. It is possible to get so carried away by enthusiasm for this new discovery that one sees parallels everywhere, even where they do not exist. Nevertheless, the pattern of biblical faith is undeniably consistent. Like the Old Testament, the New is centered in an event in history—now in the crucifixion and resurrection of this Jesus. The particularity of the cross is as inescapable as the particularity of the bondage in Egypt. It seems as scandalous to us as it did to the Jews of Paul's day, as foolish as it did to the Greeks; but the early Christians insisted on the details of time, place, and method. This death happened then and there. Outside of Jerusalem. Under Pontius Pilate. In the reign of Tiberius Caesar. And on the first day of the week, while it was yet dark. . . .

The New Testament community, like that of the Old, remembered its pivotal event. Every first day of the week became the Lord's Day, for remembering his deliverance from death on that First Easter. And the new community, too, interpreted this event as God's act. They sang in their worship of God's work in human society: "Blessed be the Lord God of Israel, for he has visited and redeemed his people." From the cross they looked back to the promises God had made to their forefathers. From the opened tomb they looked forward to the consummation of all his promises. It provided for them, as the Exodus had for their predecessors, the key to all history.

The fact that the crucifixion and resurrection of Jesus are at the center of Christian faith is still somewhat disquieting, even to second-generation, post-liberal Protestants. It apparently takes a long time to erase the after-image of a sentimentalized teacher of brotherly love. Jesus as he sat on the hillside by the Galilean lake, Jesus as he welcomed little children into his arms, Jesus in flowing blond hair as he is painted by a Sallman—these are still the favorite pictures in many Christian hearts. Mingled with the memory of crayons in Sunday school and of a piano slightly out of tune, playing "Jesus loves me, this I know, for the Bible tells me so."

If one looks to the Bible to find out what it does tell about Jesus' love, one finds a different emphasis. There is no doubt in the New Testament records about what good news the Christians had to proclaim to the first-century world. Modern scholarship has drawn our attention to passages summarizing the earliest Christian preaching, or *kerygma*. Although they are not to be taken as verbatim transcripts of sermons preached on the occasions assigned to them, the speeches attributed to Peter and to Paul in the book of Acts are good examples of this core kerygma, of what the apostolic community thought it important to say, first and foremost.

One such sermon appears in Acts 10:34-43, when Peter has been summoned to the Roman centurion Cornelius. Peter, you remember, had had a vision assuring him that such a visit to a Gentile's house, however contrary to religious custom, would not displease God. The author of Luke-Acts makes the Italian officer remind Peter that they have assembled "in the sight of God" to hear what the Lord has commanded (*10:33*). Whereupon Peter opens his mouth and delivers, not ethical exhortation nor religious philosophy, but a recital of historical event and its interpretation.

The contents of the speech can be taken as representing the primitive Christian proclamation of the good news. This eyewitness speaks about what God has done: He has anointed Jesus of Nazareth, that is, made him the Messiah, the anointed one, the Christ. Jesus went about doing good, but he was killed—by hanging on a tree. God raised him, and God made him known to those who ate and drank with him afterwards. All of this, says Peter, is what the prophets of Israel were talking about. It is according to scripture.

Another version of the same kerygma is embedded in Acts 13. This time it is Paul who speaks. Traditionally the Christian Church has read this sermon as an epistle in its

worship on Tuesday of Easter week, and the former Petrine
sermon on Monday of Easter week. In commenting on the
choice, Massey Shepherd points to the curious twist whereby
Peter was represented as speaking to the Gentile world,
whereas now Paul, the Apostle to the Gentiles, is represented
as addressing the Jewish world.[1] Paul speaks in the synagogue
in Pisidian Antioch, in Asia Minor. In keeping with one of
his major themes, the author of Acts deliberately stresses the
universality of the basic Christian story.

What does Paul have to talk about? In somewhat fuller
form, the same holy history that Peter recited. He talks about
the death and resurrection of Jesus, setting it in the context
of the Jewish past and attempting to demonstrate that this
act of the God of Israel really fulfills the divine promises. As
he had promised, God brought a Saviour to Israel. Not recognizing him, the Jews asked Pilate to have him killed. When
he was dead, they took him down from the cross and en-
tombed him. But God raised him from the dead.

In the course of his argument, Paul cites the testimony of
the psalms and of the prophet Isaiah to show how this was in
accordance with the scriptures. Such proof-texts from the Old
Testament were part of the standard equipment of early
Christian preachers commending the gospel to their fellow
Jews. Having themselves understood this new event of Jesus
in the light of their belief in God's past acts in history, they
collected passages from their scriptures which they thought
pointed toward this new act. Such a collection, oral or written,
is being drawn on here. The author has Paul clinch his argument with a quotation from the prophet Habakkuk, through
whom God declares, "I do a deed in your days."

Some aspects of this Acts version of the Christian good
news differ slightly from the characteristic Pauline interpretation of Jesus the Christ, as found in his own letters. But there
is no doubt that Paul based his proclamation on precisely
the same fact of the death and resurrection of Jesus. The

locus classicus in the letters which demonstrates Paul's dependence on the same primitive kerygma comes in I Corinthians 15, when he writes to remind those in Corinth of the terms in which he had preached the gospel to them:

For I delivered to you as of first importance what I also received, that Christ died for our sins in accordance with the scriptures, that he was buried, that he was raised on the third day in accordance with the scriptures . . . (*I Cor. 15:3-4*).

New Testament theology everywhere begins, therefore, with this datum of historical experience. Jesus was executed, but the Christians were convinced that he was alive, that God had raised him up, that they had seen him. The New Testament thinkers who explore the implications of this are individual men, each trying to speak to the needs of a special group in a particular situation. In consequence, their writings offer diversity, rather than uniformity, of interpretation. But they all reflect on the person and work of Christ from the Good Friday–Easter focal point.

THREE CHRISTOLOGICAL STATEMENTS

We shall look at three very familiar theological statements—one according to Paul, one according to John, and one according to the author of Hebrews—to indicate both the variety and the similarity of New Testament thought. Each of these statements uses a different major image to express an understanding of who Christ is.

The first in point of time occurs in St. Paul's letter to the church at Philippi. Paul has a warm affection for this group of Christians, the oldest of the European congregations he helped to found. Now in prison, he is conscious of being supported through their faith. He writes to thank them for this support and to encourage them to continue in authentic life, regardless of the fact that it will inevitably bring opposition from the established order of society. Almost in an offhand manner, he injects into a homely exposition of how Christians should behave, a pattern to follow:

Have this mind among yourselves, which you have in Christ Jesus, who, though he was in the form of God, did not count equality with God a thing to be grasped, but emptied himself, taking the form of a servant, being born in the likeness of men. And being found in human form he humbled himself, and became obedient unto death, even death on a cross. Therefore God has highly exalted him and bestowed on him the name which is above every name, that at the name of Jesus every knee should bow in heaven and on earth and under the earth, and every tongue confess that Jesus Christ is Lord, to the glory of God the Father (*Phil. 2:5-11*).

The death and resurrection, or exaltation, of Jesus Christ is clearly a key point in this recital. Reflection on its meaning has looked backward to the birth of Jesus, and behind that birth to the divine initiative which led to this life and death. The pre-existence of Christ is assumed. This is a common feature of all three christological passages we are now considering. Here he is said to have been "in the form of God."

But here also a contrasting phrase is used to describe the Christ, one which carried with it a specific set of associations. He took "the form of a servant." In using the figure of the servant, this passage points directly to a major stream of New Testament thinking about the death of Jesus for which the Old Testament had prepared the way. To the mind trained in the scriptures, as Paul's was, the figure of a servant—literally, a slave—evoked the suffering servant described by the prophet Second Isaiah. The Isaiah poems in chapters 40-55 deal profoundly with the paradox of joy through suffering, with the mystery of glory through humiliation, which were at the heart of reality as the Poet-Prophet understood it through his experience of Israel's national downfall and exile.

Instead of trying to soft-pedal the spectacular failure of Jesus—his complete humiliation and rejection—the earliest Christian theologians found it consistent with the Isaiah view of the way God is and acts. Paul is not alone in making this connection. It underlies much of the gospel tradition, particularly in St. Mark; and there is good reason to believe that Jesus himself was responsible for equating his own person and ministry with that of the suffering servant. From careful exegesis of this appearance of the theme in Philippians, some interpreters conclude that Paul was quoting a Christian psalm already well known to himself and his readers. Others think that there is insufficient evidence for such a conclusion. But whether this statement represents a previous articulation of the Faith or Paul's original expression, his use of the idea of the suffering servant is wholly in keeping with the rest of his theology. In all Paul's letters there is a forceful development of the theme of the cross. He preached Christ crucified. He determined, he says, to know nothing else. Writing now from prison, and about conflict and suffering, he thinks of Jesus in that form.

In spite of the difficulties of interpreting this passage, or perhaps because of them, it has had great theological influence in modern times. Its idea of the divine self-emptying provides a foundation for an interpretation of the person of Jesus Christ which takes its name from the Greek word for emptying used here, the word *kenosis*. A kenotic Christology suggests that Christ abandoned divine nature in order to assume human nature.[2] And yet it is clear at the end of the passage, when Paul writes about Jesus Christ as he is in the present, that he is still thinking of the divine nature of this servant. When he declares that every knee shall bow at the name of the exalted Jesus, every tongue confess him Lord, he is alluding to God's own statement in Isaiah's prophecy:

Turn to me and be saved,
  all the ends of the earth!
For I am God, and there is no other. . . .
  To me every knee shall bow,
Every tongue shall swear

                    (*Isa. 45:22-23*).

The Philippians passage referred to God the Father but it did not make direct use of the correlative idea of sonship. The image of Son is present, however, in the introduction to the anonymous letter to the Hebrews, which tradition assigns to be read as the epistle on Christmas (*Heb. 1:1-14*). We do not know who or where these "Hebrew" Christians were, but they were evidently becoming lukewarm, nominal church-men—drifting away from their first enthusiasm, shrinking back from exposure to public criticism, neglecting to meet together. We do not know for certain who or where the author was, only that he was trying to counteract this apathy (*accidie*). The first chapter as a whole deserves intensive study, with the aid of commentaries and in the context of the rest of the treatise which it introduces, but our interest at the moment is limited to the implied dimensions of the son-ship metaphor used. The first three verses of the chapter read:

In many and various ways God spoke of old to our fathers by the prophets; but in these last days he has spoken to us by a Son, whom he appointed the heir of all things, through whom also he created the world. He reflects the glory of God and bears the very stamp of his nature, upholding the universe by his word of power. When he had made purification for sins, he sat down at the right hand of the Majesty on high. . . .

There follows a catena of Old Testament quotations, chiefly from the psalms, which prove, this writer thinks, that the Son is superior by nature to any other spiritual beings in the whole angelic hierarchy presupposed by his first-century readers. The author is well acquainted with the Hebrew scriptures and accustomed to interpreting them allegorically. This kind of scriptural exegesis, which flourished in such Hellenistic cities as Alexandria, was probably more persuasive to those who knew the rules of the game than it is to us. The texts quoted so confidently do not seem to our minds to warrant all the conclusions drawn from them.

Since his readers are Christians, they have already heard and responded to the kerygma, the good news about the death and resurrection of Christ. He merely alludes to this in the opening sentences therefore—"when he had made purification for sins, he sat down at the right hand of the Majesty on high." His readers will guess what he is talking about, and in any event he is going on to discuss this in detail, explaining the purification for sins by drawing a parallel between the death of Christ and the sacrificial blood offered annually by the Jewish high priest on the Day of Atonement. He is more interested at the outset in calling attention to who effected this new, once-for-all atonement. For this purpose, he speaks of the Son of God.

The Son he has in mind is not the man Jesus as such, but primarily an eternal Son who was co-agent in the creation of the cosmos. He and other Christians found the idea of such a co-agent already present in Hebrew scriptures, in the eighth chapter of Proverbs, and in other writings dating from the Hellenistic period. This personified Wisdom here becomes the Son. The expressions used, suggesting mirrored glory and derived imprint, both identify him with and subordinate him to God.

For God to speak directly through this Son instead of through the prophets is something new, we are told. Yet the person of the Son can be, and is, explained through the old writings; and among the psalms chosen for the purpose, royal imagery figures prominently. The words "thou art my son," quoted in verse 5, are from Psalm 2, where they are addressed to the king God has set on his holy hill in Zion. The scepter and the throne (vv. 8-9) belong, in the original, to the one anointed by God as king; Psalm 45 is about a royal wedding. In their context, the verses from Psalm 102 about the Lord as creator (vv. 10-12) follow the statement that the Lord is enthroned forever. And finally, the footstool introduced from Psalm 110 (v. 13) ie a royal footstool, part of the special furniture of kingship. All these quotations are intended to support the author's previous statement that the Son is now once more at the right hand of Majesty on high. In his eyes, the coming of the Son represents the coming of the King of creation, to be made partaker of human nature.

As a third and final example of the variety of theological interpretation found in the New Testament, look at the prologue to the Fourth Gospel, John 1:1-14. It makes a fitting companion-piece to the Hebrews selection, having for centuries followed it in the hearing of the Christian community as the Gospel read on Christmas Day. It too makes use of the image of a unique Son: "we have beheld his glory, glory as of the only Son from the Father." It is also an appropriate parallel to the Philippians passage, for some scholars believe that it too is an older Christian hymn, rather than the original composition of the writer in whose work it is now included. And, like Paul's self-emptying passage, the Johannine introduction emphasizes the change in status involved in God's entry into the world.

There are notable differences, however, between this and either of the christological statements we have looked at previously. In the first place, direct or even oblique reference to the basic kerygma of crucifixion-resurrection is not so readily apparent. The historical fact of the cross undoubtedly lies behind the statements that the world knew him not, and that his own people received him not. And the Resurrection is certainly presupposed in the flat statement that the darkness has not overcome the light. Nevertheless, we have moved even further from the simple proclamation of the primitive community. Moreover, John's dependence on Old Testament ideas for clues to the meaning of the new event is far less evident than it was either in Paul's use of the servant theme or in the Hebrews' direct quotation of scripture. Instead, what is most striking and most puzzling here is the idea of the Word which became flesh and dwelt among us.

What is this Word, or *Logos*, which readers of the Fourth Gospel are supposed to know about? Is the author talking about the Logos as Greek philosophy might—particularly the Stoics, who so named the rational principle of order in the cosmos? Or is he thinking in the tradition of Hellenistic Judaism, of such a recent philosopher as Philo, the Alexandrian Jew who equates the Logos of God with the Wisdom figure present with the Creator at the beginning of his works? Is he under the sway of esoteric mythologies current in the religious thought of his day, such as those embraced by the Jewish sect of Essenes? Or again, is he more influenced by the rabbis who connected God's word and wisdom with his Torah, the revelation of his will to Israel? Would John's first readers be expected to think of one, rather than another, of these traditions when they heard, "In the beginning was the Word, and the Word was with God, and the Word was God. He was in the beginning with God; all things were made through him, and without him was not anything made that was made"?

The question is a difficult one, which has long excited students of the Fourth Gospel, and will undoubtedly continue to do so, especially as scholars find new affinities between the Fourth Gospel and the Essene theology still becoming better known to us from study of the Dead Sea Scrolls. I doubt that the author intended to give a precise content to this Word. It seems much more likely that he is deliberately using a wide-angle lens here. That in applying the word Logos to the Christ he is consciously synthesizing Jewish,

Hellenistic, and primitive Christian strands of thought.[3] In so doing, he provided the Christian intellectual world with a term which became the subject of minute analysis and heated philosophical discussion in later centuries. He himself seems primarily interested in witnessing to the fulness of life and light and grace and truth made known to men in God's action in history.

In looking at this New Testament selection in its biblical context, we would underline just one of the theological implications which its use of the Logos metaphor makes inescapable. Whether the first fourteen verses of John were freshly written as a prose introduction to this Gospel or had a previous history in Christian worship, they now stand at the beginning of a work which makes little use of the word Logos but much of the concept. They now appear in the prologue to a theological treatise which deliberately contrasts the old order and the new, the synagogue and the Church, Moses and Jesus. The law given through Moses has been superseded by the truth known through Jesus Christ (1:17). The healing powers of the bronze serpent which Moses lifted up on a pole in the wilderness are surpassed by the life-giving powers of the cross on which Jesus was lifted up (3:14, 8:28, 12:34). Once more, that is, there is pointed effort to show the discontinuity between Judaism and Christianity by means of the accepted premise of continuity—that Jesus Christ can only be explained according to the scriptures.

From this perspective, the beginning of the Fourth Gospel must inevitably be read in the light of the beginning of Genesis. Both books say: in the beginning God created. In Genesis 1, God spoke and the world came into being. He looked and saw that it was good. In the Fourth Gospel (using the translation of the New English Bible), "When all things began, the Word already was." And this Word "entered his own realm" (1:11a). In the Johannine version of New Testament thought, the doctrine of incarnation implicit here in the introduction is made explicit in the signs which Jesus does in the flesh. He turns water into wine when an emergency arises at a wedding party (2:1-11). He heals a sick child simply by speaking a word (4:46-54). He feeds a hungry crowd despite a drastically limited supply of bread and fishes (6:1-14). All these actions are offered as demonstrations of his power over the created order. As the incarnate Logos, he has this power by nature.

When the early Christian theologians reflected on the meaning of the life and death and resurrection of Jesus Christ, they all thought about who he was in the light of what he had done. They thought backward from Easter to Christmas. They did not separate his person from his work. They interpreted both his person and his work in the light of the God known to them in the history and scriptures of the people of Israel. With the help of scripture, they thought backward to a pre-existent Christ. The metaphors they used of the Christ convey both difference from and yet near identity with this God who created the universe and who acts within it to create new possibilities in human life. In talking of a Servant, a Son, a Logos, the New Testament writers provided the raw materials for future generations to use in trying to develop a rational, systematic theology—in trying to define doctrines of the incarnation or the atonement. But only the raw materials. The New Testament writers themselves looked toward another future.

CHAPTER 4

The Expectant Community

What if there is no future? The question confronts our atomic age as stark possibility. We tell horror stories about someone accidentally pushing the wrong button to start a nuclear holocaust, gruesome tales about the effects of fall-out on unborn grandchildren. Reassuring diagrams of triple-check safety measures do not really silence the stories, because this terror is not subject to rational controls. It operates in the inarticulate depths of our being.

"The shadow that the possibility of nuclear war casts over the human spirit," William Ernest Hocking said recently, "is not solely the shadow of measureless calamity. It is also a shadow over human self-respect, and over the entire scope of human faith." Writing on "The Freedom to Hope," just before his ninetieth birthday, the philosopher continues, "Nuclear war confronts faith . . . with a total negation, whether or not the group involved is our own, for it is our conception of human destiny that is at stake." He describes the atmosphere in which the youth of Western lands are growing up as one where "faith in any total meaning of the world process has become a dubious placebo." [1]

Hocking did not, I think, exaggerate the profound sense of hopelessness in American youth. His observations might not disturb one type of Christian theologian. In the name of faith, such men would welcome a shaking of faith in the idea that human action can shape the future. In the service of a Dostoevskian conviction that true faith is born only from despair, they seek to drive men to admit the inadequacy of all human action. Only when a man's back is pressed hard against the wall of human sin and impotence, they seem to believe, will he dare the leap into true faith—faith in the adequacy of divine action.

Is despair of the future a necessary prerequisite to faith? If we turn back to the Bible to explore this problem, we find strong reason to doubt it. We find indisputable evidence, at any rate, that faith in the biblical sense entails a very positive hope in the future. After all our emphasis on God's action in history, the fact should not surprise us. The biblical perspective, we have insisted, sees time as dynamic. God has acted; he will act. An orientation toward the future is one of the distinctive aspects of the biblical response to God's activity in time.

This orientation toward the future is always a community response. Biblical hopes are shared hopes. Shared by the people of God in the present, and directed toward a shared future. There is nothing private or individualistic about the future which seems most desirable to men of biblical faith. The remembering community was also an expectant community. But what was it that they expected? And what part did man play in bringing it about? Our concern in this chapter is to think of the nature and content of hope as the Bible understands it.

THE PROPHETIC HOPE

Exploration of this theme involves us in eschatology. This is another essential term in biblical theology, highly popular today, which comes from a Greek word used in the New Testament—the word *eschatos*, meaning last. Ideas of eschatology, or "last things," are not confined to a temporal future, however, any more than the English word "end" is limited to the final point in a time series. You might easily come to the end of this chapter, for example, without having reached the desired end of being provoked to think. Eschatology carries a comparable double meaning. It connotes both the terminus and the goal, and the two are not necessarily the same. Thus it is possible to encounter eschatological thought which is about ultimate things but which is not futurist.

With just this much introduction to a very large subject, let us turn to the Bible for clarification. The Old Testament writings contain two general types of community expectation—one which is properly called prophetic, and another which is apocalyptic. They are not always easily distinguished in the prophetic books as we now have them, the products of years of additions and editings; but they have quite different roots in Israel's religious history and make quite different assumptions about the shape of the future. Yet, in spite of their differences, they both agree in planting Israel's future firmly on this earth. The Old Testament expectation is not only social; it is also this-worldly. Biblical religion as a whole is not guilty of Hocking's charge that world religions seek to escape from the threat of destruction by occupying themselves with otherworldly prospects more than with kingdoms of God on earth.[2]

Prophetic faith offers no easy optimism about the future. In fact, the first clear reference we have to the distinctive idea of prophetic eschatology, to what is called the Day of the Lord, is found in the book of the prophet Amos; and Amos' chief purpose is to puncture religious complacency. The future evidently looked rosy to those in eighth-century Israel who worshiped a tamed god. To sleek and well-fed worshipers in his age of prosperity, some twenty-eight centuries ago, Amos addressed this oracle:

> Woe to you who desire the day of the Lord!
>   Why would you have the day of the Lord?
> It is darkness, and not light
>
> > *(Amos 5:18)*.

Amos is insisting that men have a responsible share in determining the future. The Day will be dark because the businessmen of Israel trample the head of the poor into the dust (2:7), because they are willing to sell the needy for a pair of shoes (2:6). The Day will be dark, because their wives condone this attitude, egging their husbands on to bring home more money for more bowls of wine to drink, stretched on ivory couches (4:1, 6:4). Amos is certain that as long as men and women permit social injustice, the Lord cannot bring a day of light—no matter how much people enjoy their fine religious services. Under the circumstances, their religiosity only makes the coming Day darker. When one excises the blatantly hopeful passage added by a later hand, the book of Amos ends with unequivocal negation:

> Behold, the eyes of the Lord God
>   are upon the sinful kingdom,
> and I will destroy it from the surface
>   of the ground
>
> > *(9:8)*.

The major prophets after Amos are fully as scathing as he in their indictment of the economic and social injustices in their culture, of people who serve the Lord in the temple but not in the market place. Of people who go to the temple to cry, "Peace! Peace!" when there is no peace in the land. But none of them comes as close as Amos to sounding hopeless about the future, for each of them is speaking to an age already anxious. Their people have good cause to be worried about the future, as first the Assyrians and then the Babylonians threaten the very existence of their nation. In their reading of current events, men like Hosea, Isaiah, Micah, and Jeremiah see the facts of foreign aggression and foreign domination as God's rightful judgment on the sins of his chosen people: "Ah, Assyria the rod of my anger!" (*Isa. 10:5*). But they come also to see the future Day of the Lord in corresponding but opposite terms, as a day not of war but of peace.

Out of the destruction of Israel and Judah, and out of the ensuing years of political exile in a strange land, are born prophetic hopes for a coming golden age of political independence, not unlike the remembered golden age of imperial splendor under King David. The new age will be brought about by the Lord of Israel. The exiles will be returned to the land of Israel. True worship of the Lord will be restored in his rebuilt temple at Jerusalem. True knowledge of the Lord will emanate from that holy hill. Out of the blackest days in Israel's history, the prophetic vision speaks in confidence of what the Lord will do through his people:

> . . . it shall come to pass in the latter days
>   that the mountain of the house of the Lord
> shall be established as the highest of the
>   mountains. . . .
> and all the nations shall flow to it,
>   and many peoples shall come, and say:
> "Come, let us go up to the mountain of the Lord,
>   to the house of the God of Jacob;
> that he may teach us his ways
>   and that we may walk in his paths"
>
> (*Isa. 2:2-3*).

It is only from this eschatological context that the prophets provide a motto for the United Nations building in New York. For the same oracle, now found both in Isaiah and in Micah, continues:

> He shall judge between the nations,
> and shall decide for many peoples;
> and they shall beat their swords into
> plowshares,
> and their spears into pruning hooks;
> nation shall not lift up sword against nation,
> neither shall they learn war
> any more
>
> (*Isa. 2:4; Mic. 4:1-3*).

The picture of the peaceable kingdom is painted in different colors, and varies in detail, from prophet to prophet and from age to age; but two features are constant. First, the coming days remain the Day of the *Lord*. However vague and mysterious the ideas of how or when the Day will come, God is always the chief agent in bringing it about. And yet, secondly and at the same time, the coming days cast the community of God's people in an active role. What is accomplished in the future depends in part on human responsibility. It is mediated through the people, or through that remnant of people which returns to lean upon the Lord, the Holy One of Israel.

In some—but only in some—of the prophetic thinking there is also the correlative idea that the coming reign of the Lord will be mediated through a restored monarchy, and specifically through a king of the Davidic dynasty, who will sit once more on the throne in Judah. Such messianic hopes became particularly vivid in the period of Persian domination, after Cyrus had permitted the exiles to return to their homeland, and after his successor Darius had appointed a governor who was actually a member of the old royal family.

This type of messianic expectancy was also rooted in earthly reality, albeit a species of political optimism. But the optimism, once more, came from confidence in God's continued care for his people.

Both strains of prophetic eschatology—with and without a messiah—are presently to be found together in the verses from the twenty-third chapter of the book of Jeremiah, which are appointed in the Book of Common Prayer as an epistle for the Sunday next before Advent. The passage contains two originally independent oracles, one expressing the general hope for the restoration of the nation after its destruction (*vv. 7-8*) and one expressing the particular hope that this nation will be ruled by God's anointed one (*vv. 5-6*). The responsible role of the Davidic king is clear, along with his total dependence on the Lord:

Behold, the days are coming, says the Lord, when I will raise up for David a righteous Branch, and he shall reign as king and deal wisely, and shall execute justice and righteousness in the land. In his days Judah will be saved, and Israel will dwell securely. And this is the name by which he will be called: "The Lord is our righteousness" (*Jer. 23:5-6*).

APOCALYPTIC THOUGHT

In contrast to the prophetic hope, apocalyptic thought leaves little room for human responsibility in determining the future, or for human participation in establishing it. An apocalypse undertakes to unveil the divine plans for direct intervention in human affairs; the word *apocalypse* means unveiling. On the historical level, one could argue that this type of eschatology only develops when things get even blacker for Israel—when new miseries seem to discredit the earlier prophetic hopes. Certainly the real-life situation in the second century B.C. which produced the book of Daniel, the major apocalyptic writing in the Old Testament, was a triumph of tyranny and oppression rather than of justice and righteousness. The Seleucid successor of Alexander the Great who ruled Palestine from Syria at the time was the kind of erratic despot who earned for himself the nickname "madman"; his calculated effort to stamp out Judaism had all the marks of sadism associated with later anti-Semitic tyrants. What hope was there for Israel's future?

The apocalyptic answer is a kind of determinism, which shows the influence of oriental thought. This earth is believed to be temporarily under the sway of evil powers. The only hope is in a divine intrusion into history—an end to history in the ordinary sense. Visions of "the time of the end" multiply under such persecution, and they yield elaborate blueprints of the final days. A cosmic battle must soon take place between good and evil. The combat will be between armies of angelic beings who personify both forces. The outcome is assured, however: good must conquer. The new postwar age will be ruled from victorious heaven itself. The book of Daniel describes the divinely appointed ruler in these terms:

I saw in the night visions, and behold, with the clouds of heaven there came one like a son of man, and he came to the Ancient of Days and was presented before him. And to him was given dominion and glory and kingdom, that all peoples, nations, and languages should serve him; his dominion is an everlasting dominion, which shall not pass away, and his kingdom one that shall not be destroyed (7:13-14).

The same kind of thinking is found in other places in the Old Testament. It is found in the New Testament as well. It appealed to the Christian community under the later Roman tyranny, and therefore found expression in that book known as "The Apocalypse," or The Revelation to John. His visions on the island of Patmos are an unveiling of the future in the same form as in Daniel, with all the bizarre imagery characteristic of this literary genre.

It is difficult to come to terms with apocalyptic. For the most part contemporary Christians choose to ignore it completely. What real hope for the future can twentieth-century man find in a war in heaven, with Michael and his angels fighting against the dragon? Only fanatic sectarians, we feel, can take this very seriously—the sort of fanatics whom Christian history produces at regular intervals, who calculate the date of the coming End (there are plenty of numerical clues to decode in the apocalyptic books), put on their white robes, and climb trees to wait. Or who modernize their waiting by going into a bomb shelter instead, as one sectarian group did not long ago.

One can raise the question of the relevance of apocalyptic much more easily than one can answer it.[3] One way of dealing with it is to conclude that it is only a minor strand of biblical eschatology, and thus to explain it away on the grounds provided above—that it is imported into biblical thought from alien sources, by men who were up against such overwhelming odds that they despaired of doing anything themselves to change the situation. There is much truth in this account, but it has two major weaknesses.

In the first place, it ignores the positive theological affirmations common to both prophetic and apocalyptic eschatology. Both see God as the prime author of the outcome of history and the prime hope of men in history. Both relate the End to this earth, and both describe it in community terms. Although the picture has changed from the kingdom to the city, this is as clear in the New Testament Apocalypse as it was in the Danielic vision quoted above:

Then I saw a new heaven and a new earth; for the first heaven and the first earth had passed away, and the sea was no more. And I saw the holy city, new Jerusalem, coming down out of heaven from God. . . . And I heard a great voice from the throne saying, "Behold, the dwelling of God is with men. He will dwell with them, and they shall be his people. . . ." (*Rev. 21:1-3*)

The second, and much more serious, difficulty with trying to explain away apocalyptic thought is that it has affected not only the book of Revelation but the whole New Testament. If one is trying to be faithful to biblical thought, it cannot be dismissed this lightly. All Christian hope and Christian eschatology are influenced by it. And to say this is to say that it is an integral part of Christianity. For, as the distinguished New Testament theologian Rudolf Bultmann observes, "it has become more and more clear that the eschatological expectation and hope is the core of the New Testament preaching throughout." [4]

New Testament scholars are agreed that the kingdom of God was the heart of Jesus' own teaching, and that his conception of the kingdom of God was an eschatological one. He taught his disciples to pray, "Thy kingdom come." His own preaching probably did not include the detailed pictures of the eschatological drama typical in apocalyptic literature, [5] but that of the early Christian community certainly did. Each of the first three Gospels includes unadulterated apocalyptic, such as that in the thirteenth chapter of St. Mark, where the Danielic imagery comes from the lips of Jesus. Some of the early Church, at any rate, expected the kingdom of God to come in the immediate future, with all the expected signs of the time of the End.

THE NATURE OF CHRISTIAN HOPE

Did all early Christians share this thinking? The question points to a continuing debate among contemporary interpreters of the New Testament, a debate which testifies to a polarity and tension in the New Testament documents themselves. We are aware already of the diversity of thinking in these sources. This diversity lends support to two different emphases in explaining the nature and content of Christian hope.

One school of interpretation, often associated with Bultmann's name, stresses the futurist eschatology found in all levels of the New Testament. The Church expected the imminent return of the risen Lord, to usher in the kingdom of God. In fact, as Paul's letters show, some of the early Christians even gave up their jobs to wait for his coming—causing financial problems (to say nothing of theological difficulties) when this advent, or *parousia,* was delayed. When we hear the selections from Paul's letters read in the Advent season, we are apt to forget that Christians in the middle of the first century heard them literally: "For salvation is nearer to us now than when we first believed; the night is far gone, the day is at hand" (*Rom. 13:11-12*). "Therefore do not pronounce judgment before the time, before the Lord comes" (*I Cor. 4:5*). "The Lord is at hand" (*Phil. 4:5*). The cry "Maranatha!" ("Our Lord, come!") with which Paul ended his first letter to the Corinthians was probably already a part of their regular worship. They lived in intense expectancy.

At the same time, the earliest community believed that God's Messiah had come. Jesus, the Christ, was interpreted as the fulfillment of the Old Testament hopes. As the Bethlehem birth stories so clearly indicate, he was identified with the promised Davidic king of prophetic expectation. He was also identified with the heavenly Son of Man promised in the apocalyptic literature. Both strains of eschatological thought were drawn upon in explaining who had been crucified and raised from the dead. Thus the idea of a "realized eschatology" also finds much support in the New Testament writings. The phrase is associated with the British biblical scholar C. H. Dodd and his followers, who emphasize this other pole of early Christian thought. With the coming of Jesus, it was possible to say, "the kingdom of God *is* in the midst of you" (*Luke 17:21*). Since Jesus cast out demons by God's power, then it meant that "the kingdom of God *has* come upon you" (*Luke 11:20*). The community of those who recognized the Messiah was already living in the time of the End; it was a colonial outpost of the heavenly kingdom (cf. *Phil. 3:20*).

This tension between the past and the future in New Testament thought lent a tremendous sense of urgency to the present. The early Christians were conscious of living between the times. To use the helpful if dated analogy of one commentator,[6] they had already experienced D-Day. In the death and resurrection of Jesus, the decisive battle had been fought and won. V-Day was yet to come. The ultimate victory was assured, and so the Christians could rejoice in hope. They did not have to be anxious about the outcome. But the war was not yet over. Not everyone was yet able to recognize the true significance of what had occurred. The victory parade remained for the future. In the meantime, what mattered was the now. Now is the time for the expectant community to act.

CHAPTER 5

The Response of the People of God

Biblical ethics cannot be separated from biblical theology. What the Bible calls upon men to do in the present is always dependent upon what biblical faith believes God has already done in the past and will do in the future. For this reason, the biblical imperative is introduced characteristically by a "therefore." The ethics of the Bible are an ethics of response.

THE CHURCH AS THE PEOPLE OF GOD

Next to God, the chief actor in the Bible is the people of God. Biblical thought, as we have seen, is irreducibly social. The community remembers. The community hopes. The community also acts. Biblical theologians today are intensely aware of this collective quality of thought in their sources; and their awareness has contributed greatly to one of the most notable developments on the theological scene in the last twenty-five years—a renewed interest in the idea of the Church. If, in biblical terms, the community is to act in the urgent now, then understanding of this action depends on prior understanding of this community. The Church and its mission belong together, in that order.

Children are sometimes taught to think of Pentecost, commonly called Whitsunday, as the birthday of the Church. On that day the Christian community remembers what happened to the disciples of Jesus some fifty days after the Resurrection. St. Luke's account of what happened, recorded in the second chapter of the book of The Acts of the Apostles, is read as part of the celebration of that festival. This Lukan narrative is a good starting place, therefore, in thinking about New Testament ideas of the Church.

The story itself is a strange one. A Jerusalem crowd accuses the apostles of being drunk at nine o'clock in the morning. Peter and, after him, the narrator have other interpretations of whatever unconventional behavior gave rise to the charge. Peter's explanation implies that they *were* speaking unintelligibly, but that this was ecstatic behavior induced by the gift of prophecy, not by the effects of new wine. Luke, on the other hand, insists that the speaking was perfectly intelligible, extraordinarily so. Each person in that polyglot crowd understood what was said as if the apostles were speaking directly to him, neither in prophetic gibberish nor in alcoholic Aramaic, but in his own native tongue.

The discrepancy in the narrative as it stands is not particularly important. It reflects both the tenacity of oral tradition and the particular editorial concerns of the writer. Tradition remembers *glossolalia,* or that speaking in tongues, which some early Christians certainly practiced. The writer includes the incident as he found it in the tradition, but uses it to make a different point altogether. The implications of the narrative for the self-understanding of the early Church are of greater interest. Once again, it is apparent that their self-understanding involved both a sense of continuity with the old Israel and an excited sense of newness.

The old Israel understood itself as a community called into being by God's action. One of the clearest expressions of this idea is found in the Exodus account of making the covenant at Sinai. Speaking to Moses out of the mountain, the Lord first reminds him, "You have seen what I did to the Egyptians and how I bore you on eagles' wings and brought you to myself" (*Ex. 19:4*). The "therefore" follows. Therefore you shall obey my voice; therefore you shall be a holy nation.

The Christian Church likewise understood itself to be created by God's action. Aware of the continuity of the mighty works of God, the Christians took to themselves the titles of the old Israel. The New Testament book attributed to Peter addresses the new community in language virtually identical with that of Exodus: "You are a chosen race, a royal priesthood, a holy nation, God's own people, that you may declare the wonderful deeds of him who called you out of darkness into his marvelous light" (*I Pet. 2:9*). Here in Acts also, Peter turns to scripture to interpret what is happening. He finds the answer in the book of the prophet Joel, and quotes from it at length. This strange early-morning incident is anticipated there.

Another aspect of community continuity in the Acts narrative becomes apparent only when we remember what day it was. Pentecost is not just "the birthday of the Christian Church." It was an old, long-established Jewish festival. The men who heard the apostles that morning had come to Jerusalem from all over the Roman world—from Asia, from Africa, and from Europe, according to Luke's list of the provinces represented. He suggests that they lived there, but it would have been perfectly in accord with custom for devout Jews living in the diaspora to travel to the holy center of

Judaism just to worship in the temple on this special occasion. Although Pentecost, along with the other great Jewish holidays, was originally an agricultural festival, it too had been historicized. When Luke is writing, it is the Season of the Giving of the Law, the time of remembering God's gift to his people at Sinai. The worshipers are therefore thinking already about Torah—not a restrictive legal code in Jewish thought, but a truly liberating gift, making God's will known and providing guidance for men's lives. From the Judaism of which it was then a part, the new Christian community inherited the conviction that God's action created the community. It inherited also the conviction that God guides the community which he creates.

In this context, the newness of Christian self-understanding in the Acts account appears both smaller in quantity and greater in theological importance. Luke is making deliberate contrasts. Ages ago at Sinai, God had given his Torah on this day. Today he gives his Holy Spirit. Henceforth he guides his community not merely by his revealed will. He guides it by his personal presence in its midst. A personal doctrine of the Holy Spirit is not yet fully developed here in Acts; the emphasis is rather on an outpouring of divine power. The last days have come. But later Christians rightly look to the Pentecost event as evidence of the new mode of God's presence with his people, bringing with it new power for action in the world.

By bothering to include so much geography, Luke invites a second contrast between the two communities. Here and in all his writing, he insists that the Church is universal in scope, as Israel was not. Jerusalem is the starting point, but the community spreads out from there into all the world. Citizens from all nations—east and west, north and south— are there to witness what is happening. They ask what it means. Peter answers with God's promise from Joel: "And it shall be that whoever calls on the name of the Lord shall be saved" (*v. 21*). In Lukan theology, universalism is a keynote of the new community. This is the catholic Church.

THE CHURCH AS THE BODY OF CHRIST

The New Testament speaks about the Church in another way which has had a tremendous influence on the community's later thinking about itself. It calls the Church the Body of Christ. Many different figures of speech express many ideas of the *Ekklesia,* the assembly of the people, in the New Testament writings. The metaphor of the body is especially prominent only in four Pauline letters—First Corinthians, Romans, Colossians, and Ephesians. Indeed, it has so little importance elsewhere in the New Testament that contemporary writers are properly outspoken against using it as the only basis for a theology of the Church. Happily, they are re-emphasizing some of the other New Testament ways of thinking and speaking about God's people. Nevertheless, the body image has been used so much (and often so glibly) that it deserves our special attention.

In the four letters cited, the word *body* occurs more than seventy times. By no means is it always applied to the community, however. The Greek word for body (*soma*) has much the same versatility that the English word has. Its richness of meaning comes to mind if we just think quickly of the body politic, the student body, the body beautiful, the body by Fisher, the dead body on the library floor. In Paul's day, the word had special associations in Stoic thought, so that part of his enthusiasm for the word in its collective sense may stem from the apologetic purpose of speaking in terms that his readers would be sure to understand. They were already accustomed to thinking of the political world as a great body with the ruler at its head. He may also have been influenced by polemic motives, arguing indirectly against a bifurcation of reality which led to downgrading the human body.

Paul is also aware of the specific references the word already carried in Christian tradition. He hands on to the church in Corinth the eucharistic words of Jesus as he had received them: "This is my body which is for you" (*I Cor. 11:24*). He discusses with the puzzled Corinthians the problems of the resurrection body. As Christ had been raised bodily from the dead, so too will they be raised. This is of first importance in the received tradition. But their confusion about the mechanics of the resurrection will be cleared up if they just remember that the word *body* is not limited in meaning to one kind of physical body (*I Cor. 15*).

Paul, then, is fully conscious of the shifting connotations, of the clusters of meanings conveyed by the word he chooses to describe for the Corinthians the nature of the Christian community:

For just as the body is one and has many members, and all the members of the body, though many, are one body, so it is with Christ. For by one Spirit we were all baptized into one body—Jews or Greeks, slaves or free—and all were made to drink of one Spirit. . . . Now you are the body of Christ and individually members of it" (*I Cor. 12:12-13, 27*).

In his sustained treatment of the Church as the Body of Christ, between verses 12 and 27, Paul is clearly stressing the unity of "the church of God which is at Corinth"—a unity which cannot be dissolved by their current bickerings over which human leader baptized them or which delivers more impressive sermons. He is trying to make them realize their interdependence and mutual responsibility in the Church, even if some people do seem more gifted than others. Different capabilities mean different jobs to do. This diversity is as natural in the community as it is in the individual human organism. But in both cases, the parts function in behalf of the whole; and all of them are vital to its health.

At the end of his letter to the church at Rome, Paul makes exactly the same point. When he turns from theological exposition to deal directly with the ethical consequences of what he has been saying, he begins: "I appeal to you, *therefore*, brethren. . . ." (*Rom. 12:1*). He then enjoins them to offer their *bodies* as a living sacrifice, calling this the true spiritual work and worship of Christians. And he immediately thinks again of the one body: "For as in one body we have many members, and all the members do not have the same function, so we, though many, are one body in Christ, and individually members one of another" (*Rom. 12:4-5*). This Romans passage adds little to the understanding of the Church suggested in its Corinthians parallel until one notices that Paul has already used the word *body* ten times in the earlier part of the Romans letter, and that nine of the times the word was conspicuously linked with sin and death.[1] Collectively or singly, bodies are not necessarily good things in Paul's mind. There is an essential ambiguity in the term itself. In and of themselves, bodies are not immortal. To be a created body means to die.

In its Romans context, the distinctive thing about the Body of Christ is that it dies and is raised again. To belong to this body is to participate in the death as well as in the resurrection of the Lord: "Likewise, my brethren, you have died to the law through the body of Christ, so that you may belong to another, to him who has been raised from the dead in order that we may bear fruit for God" (*7:4*). Or again, in the same vein, "Do you not know that all of us who have been baptized into Christ Jesus were baptized into his death? We were buried therefore with him by baptism into death, so that as Christ was raised from the dead by the glory of the Father, we too might walk in newness of life" (*6:3-4*). All of this lies behind Paul's injunction to his brethren to present therefore their bodies as a sacrifice, since they are "one body in Christ and individually members one of another."

These closely interwoven ideas invoked by the body metaphor recur in Paul's letter to the Colossians and in the very similar letter to the Ephesians. But in these writings still another feature of the Church comes into bold relief. The Church is the body; Christ is its head. In Colossians the declaration is straightforward and simple: "He is the head of the body, the church" (*1:18*). Elaboration of the same metaphor in Ephesians 4 presents a more complicated picture. There is one body. The body has diversity of gifts among the members. But all are to grow up in every way "into him who is the head, into Christ, from whom the whole body, joined and knit together by every joint with which it is supplied, when each part is working properly, makes bodily growth and upbuilds itself in love" (*Eph. 4:15-16*). It would be difficult to diagram the sentence or the organism, but its theological implications are plain enough. The Church is subordinate to its head, Jesus Christ, and dependent on him for its growth and development.

From all three ways in which the body image is used—to stress diversified unity, sacrificial death, or derivative power—we must conclude that in Pauline thought the Church and its members are defined in this way with central reference to Jesus Christ. His body was crucified and raised again. His broken body is shared with his Church. Believers are made members of his body by baptism into his death, a baptism which delivers them from what Paul calls the body of sin, and incorporates them into his new life. The body so defined is closely knit together in organic interdependence of its parts, but in total dependence on the head.

WORSHIP AND ETHICS

From the Acts account of Pentecost, we found that the people of God are called out to be the Spirit-filled community. In the Pauline letters, they are called to be this Body of Christ. Both types of New Testament thinking about the Church mean that the vocation of the community is primarily to new being. But in response to this new being, they are called to act with power. What are they called to do? The biblical writers have many very specific things to say on the subject. They are speaking to their own age, and not directly to our situation as the Church in the modern world. We are not, for example, greatly bothered by whether or not we should patronize butcher shops selling meat previously offered to idols in pagan temples. Advice meant to help with that particular problem cannot be allegorized or spiritualized without violating the historical character of the biblical documents.

But whether we look at what the earliest Christian writers told the community they ought to do, or look at what they tell us the community in fact did do, we cannot help noticing two constant principles: *Eucharist* and *agape*, thanksgiving and overflowing love, go together in the response of the New Testament community. Worship and ethics are two sides of the same coin.

At the end of the second chapter of Acts, which begins with the Pentecost event, the life of the new community is summarized in these words:

And all who believed were together and had all things in common; and they sold their possessions and goods and distributed them to all, as any had need. And day by day, attending the temple together and breaking bread in their homes, they partook of food with glad and generous hearts, praising God and having favor with all the people (*2:44-47*).

Undoubtedly an idealized picture, as later incidents in the same book indicate; but nevertheless a revealing one. The primitive breaking of bread in eucharistic action has been joined to the traditional worship of the temple as an everyday form of praising God. The glad hearts of the believers impel them also to minister directly and practically to the needs of others.

The end section of Romans began in chapter 12, as we saw, with a declaration of the same interrelationship. There, spiritual worship is to be expressed in bodily terms of sacrificial proportions. Christian self-giving is always, as it were, in two directions. Paul spells out the reasonable, holy, and living sacrifice of Christians in a series of ethical injunctions which include every aspect of life, from paying taxes to putting up with the idiosyncracies of other peoples' diets. The imperative to pray and the imperative to contribute to human needs come side by side. And he sums up all he has been saying by quoting the Lord's command to love. This is the present mission of the people of God in all the world.

It is fitting to remember, finally, that for New Testament thought the arena of loving action in the present is outside the walls of the holy city, as well as in. As the author of Hebrews puts it, "So Jesus also suffered outside the gate. . . . *Therefore* let us go forth to him outside the camp, bearing abuse for him" (*Heb. 13:12-13*). Or, in the closely connected thought of St. Luke, expressed through the words of the risen Lord: "Thus it is written, that the Christ should suffer and on the third day rise from the dead, and that repentance and forgiveness of sins should be preached in his name to all nations, *beginning* from Jerusalem. You are witnesses of these things" (*Lk. 24:46-48*).

PART II
DIALOGUES WITH TRADITION

CHAPTER 6

Matter and Spirit

There is no a priori reason to believe that the God who makes himself known in history abruptly stopped doing so sometime in the middle of the second century. Christian history is a continuum. The God who made himself known to Israel made himself known also to the community which called itself the New Israel. That new community used the same Bible as the old, but it also produced numerous writings of its own. By the end of the second century, it had selected some of them to put alongside of the old scriptures as the New Testament. But even though the Church adopted no later writings as Holy Scripture, it believed that God was still active in its affairs. It still believes this.

THE TRADITION OF THE CHURCH

For this reason, tradition makes a claim on the minds of thinking Christians. The continuity of the theological enterprise is part of the continuity of the Church. Richard Niebuhr rightly reminds us that the definition of revelation is a social task of the historic Christian community and that we stand at a limited point in the life of that community. Our effort to define grows out of a struggle with the problems of the past; it is one effort among many others in the present, and it leads into future phases of a continuing conversation. Any present definition of the central element will need to be tested by an historical theology. . . .[1]

The results of historical research in the last decades reinforce the theological grounds for this perspective. We are in a better position than our forefathers to realize that the New Testament is indeed a community product, not just the independent work of a few apostles turned author. We know, too, that there was considerable debate in the early Church about which writings were to be considered normative, or canonical. In fact, the earliest list of New Testament writings which has come down to us in exactly the form of our present table of contents is found in the Easter letter written to his diocese by Athanasius, the Bishop of Alexandria, in 367.

Prior to that time, some Christian writings which did not finally win a place among the canonical literature were so popular in certain locales that they were read aloud in public worship. Others, which did make it into the Canon—largely on the basis of supposed apostolic authorship—were criticized elsewhere as inferior in style or suspect in doctrine. Centuries later even Martin Luther, probably the most outspoken proponent of the authority of scripture in Christian history, dubbed the letter of James an "epistle of straw." By rejecting the ideas in that New Testament book, he demonstrates that the decisions of the Church in choosing its Holy Scripture are not necessarily accepted as infallible.

There is no need to depreciate the value of the Canon in order to insist on the importance of non-canonical and post-canonical writings, however. The sphere of tradition in the Christian Church involves the total thought and practice of the Church through the centuries—the whole experience of the living, ongoing community. One cannot point arbitrarily to any date in history and say, "Thus far and no farther will I listen to the past." The decisions of the Councils in the period of the so-called undivided Church (which in fact knew many divisions) may have a greater claim to authority in Christian thought than the decisions of later and lesser councils; but this does not mean that theologians of later ages are of lesser stature or significance than the fathers of Nicea or Chalcedon.

In sixteenth-century debate with the Puritans, Anglican leaders rose to the defense of tradition, along with scripture, as an authoritative guide for Christian thought and practice. One of the most gifted spokesmen in this debate, Richard Hooker, fully recognized the pre-eminence of scripture; but he made a telling point for the voice of Christian history as well when he wrote, "St. Augustine exhorteth not to hear men, but to hearken what God speaketh. His purpose is not (I think) that we should stop our ears against his own exhortation." [2] Hooker's basis for the defense of tradition was, again, a theological one:

But whom God hath endued with principal gifts to aspire unto knowledge by; whose exercises, labours, and divine studies he hath so blessed that the world for their great and rare skill that way hath them in singular admiration; may we reject even their judgment likewise, as being utterly of no moment? For mine own part, I dare not so lightly esteem of the Church, and of the principal pillars therein. [3]

Very few of these principal pillars whom Hooker and his age esteemed were armchair theologians. Most of them were on the front lines in the intellectual battles of their own day. Their writings are not abstract theoretical treatises, but rather thoroughly practical in intent, occasioned by the problems of current affairs. The fathers of the Church—and there is no need to limit the term to the early centuries which the textbooks call the patristic period—were active churchmen, actively involved in their own time and place. To understand their thought, one must see them in the context of their own culture fully as much as is the case of the biblical writers.

But when one looks at the "occasional theology" of the past in full recognition of that same historical particularity which applies to biblical theology, one finds that they were engrossed with questions which are still living questions in our own day. As thinking Christians they faced their own culture, even as we must. And the problems they found there for thought, the answers they gave, illumine our problems and our answers. In this section, therefore, five successive periods in the life of the Church have been selected to join the continuing conversation about five different questions of contemporary theology. The first is the post-apostolic age, which confronted a culture greatly interested in ideas about matter and spirit.

THE GNOSTIC REJECTION OF MATERIALISM

A curious confusion clouds our thinking about the material universe today. On the one hand, we in the West are officially at war with a philosophy of materialism, so that the word itself increasingly invites the epithet "Marxian." At the same time, another kind of materialism pervades our way of life. The discoveries and achievements of modern science have gradually filtered down into the popular consciousness in such a way that we are subtly persuaded to consider physical energy the master reality. And even where this conclusion is most stoutly denied on the philosophical level, our advertisers conspire to make materialists of us on the behavioral level. Secular materialism prevails in fact, if not in theory.

Against all forms of materialist thinking, American religiosity reacts overtly with a fervent but fuzzy spiritualism. Dialectical and secular materialism alike evoke talk of "the spiritual realm," wherever or whatever that may be—its champions can seldom say. Naïve scientism and its Madison Avenue cousin provoke an equally naïve defense of something called "spiritual values." As part of this reaction, any religious position which seems to prefer non-material reality attracts respectful attention. The recent interest in Zen Buddhism is but one example of this tendency; and it is noteworthy that the Zen of the faddist was usually denuded of its demand for discipline.

In the Christian churches there seems to be little clear thinking either about the nature of the material world or about its value. Our economy of abundance, as one commentator acutely observes, is producing a moral revolution such that the old thrift-oriented ethic of Protestantism is giving way to a "new mentality of happily wasteful indulgence";[4] but we seem unprepared to cope realistically with this revolution. All too often the Christian finds himself merely caught in ambivalence. Spiritual, not material, reality is ultimate, he insists. But material things are somehow worth more than society allows: there is something fundamentally wrong, he feels, about the auto graveyards dotting our countryside, about the wastebaskets full of junk mail and supermarket packaging.

Why? What is the relationship between spirit and matter? What is the right attitude toward the things we are preoccupied with and tyrannized by? Similar questions confronted the Christians of the second century with an intellectual crisis of major proportions, when an extremely attractive religious philosophy known as *gnosticism* captured the minds of many both without and within the Church. Leading churchmen did battle against it with all their mental powers, but it was not easily defeated. Gnosticism, which the later Church called a heresy, has strange affinities with present-day religious reactions against materialism.

For many years our knowledge of this early rival to Christianity was drawn chiefly from Christian polemic against it. In 1945, however, near the Egyptian town of Nag Hammadi, a gnostic library was discovered, awakening new interest in the subject and providing fresh source materials for its study. The importance of the find for knowledge of the Christian past is equal to that of the Dead Sea Scrolls, even though it received less attention in the popular press. In a large earthenware jar, some peasants found thirteen leather-bound volumes, containing forty-four different documents written in Coptic on papyrus sheets.

Conflicting stories are told about how the peasants disposed of their find, including the historian's nightmare that they used some of the sheets to start a fire for their tea water; but it is certain that most of the manuscripts eventually found their way into the Coptic Museum in Cairo. The remaining codex fell into the hands of a Belgian antiquities dealer, from whom it was purchased as an eightieth birthday present for the Swiss psychologist Carl Jung. This Jung Codex contains a document called "The Gospel of Truth." Uncomplimentary references to a gnostic work of the same title appear in the writings of the second-century Christian theologian Irenaeus; and although the Nag Hammadi documents in their present form date from the fourth century, scholars have little doubt that this is a version of the same gospel. Other items in the collection, such as "The Gospel of Thomas" and "The Gospel of Philip," are gradually being translated into English and made available to the general public.[5]

Detailed study of this gnostic library is far from complete, some twenty years after the original discovery; but in general the documents support the previous picture of the movement

drawn from the church fathers and from a few extant fragments of pro-gnostic writings. It is easy to oversimplify
gnosticism. Rival sects existed as followers of one or another
popular gnostic teacher; there were pagan, Jewish, and Christian varieties. Whatever their peculiarities, however, all gnostics shared a dualistic metaphysics and as a result had similar
approaches to ethics.

As its more familiar cognate *agnosticism* suggests, the
term gnosticism comes from the Greek word *gnosis,* knowledge. As a religion, it purported to give its adherents secret
knowledge of the true way of salvation. Related ultimately
to an oriental dualism, it believed that spirit is good but that
the material universe is evil. Theories about the origins of the
world are clothed in elaborate myths imparted to the elite as
part of their liberating *gnosis,* and differ from sect to sect.
Salvation consists in freeing one's spiritual nature from control by the material nexus, in rescuing the divine spark in
man from imprisonment in matter. Rosicrucians and other
occult groups today are direct descendants of the gnostics;
Christian Scientists share many of their views. But so, too,
does much of the spiritualism within "orthodox" Christian
groups.

When one believes that material things, including the
physical body, are either evil or illusory, two quite opposite
attitudes toward them are possible. On the one hand, one
can logically decide that they are therefore insignificant, that
what one does with his body, for example, is of no great importance. This results in an ethical indifference, the position
of the antinomian, who is above the law. On the other hand,
with equal logic, one can decide that the physical side of his
life must be rigidly controlled, and adopt all sorts of ascetic
practices to insure the mastery of the material by the spiritual.
Groups properly described as gnostic apparently espoused
both ethical viewpoints in the second century.

GNOSTICISM AND THE INCARNATION

For the Christian gnostic, or for Christians influenced by gnostic thought, the man Jesus of Nazareth was an embarrassment. The idea of the Incarnation is a fundamental contradiction to their devaluation of the physical universe. It is unseemly, if not unthinkable, to assert that the Saviour of the world became flesh and dwelt among men as real man. A human birth and particularly an ignominious, suffering death were not appropriate means to adopt in order to liberate men from the evils of physical birth, life, and death. Accordingly, very early in the Church's life, an interpretation of Christ developed which asserted that he did not really suffer and die, that he only appeared to do so. This is the position known as *docetism*, from the Greek word for appear, or seem. Jesus' Passion was all play-acting, a grand illusion.

Argument against gnostic philosophy and ethics, and against the related christological ideas of docetism, can be detected within the New Testament itself. Apart from the New Testament writers, one of the earliest and strongest opponents of this thought-world was Ignatius, second-century Bishop of Antioch in Syria. His thinking is preserved only in seven letters he wrote about A.D. 115, while traveling across Asia Minor under military escort en route to martyrdom in Rome. The letters are intensely personal, even passionate, documents written to convey thanks and advice to the churches which sent delegations to honor and comfort him along the march. Under the circumstances, one cannot expect to find in them lengthy discourse or reasoned refutation of gnostic thought; and one does not. The essential Christian counteraffirmations against gnosticizing tendencies, however, are clearly spelled out in Ignatius' letters.

A delegation from Ephesus had reported to Ignatius that itinerant teachers were visiting their congregation, advocating

new ideas. They complained that some of their members
flaunted the name of Christian without acting accordingly.
Ignatius compares such men to mad dogs whose bite must be
avoided because it is so hard to heal. The only physician for
such bites, he remarks, is Jesus Christ

of flesh, yet spiritual, born yet unbegotten, God incarnate, genuine life in the midst of death, sprung from Mary as well as God,
first subject to suffering then beyond it. . . .[6]

He seems almost to be reciting the phrases from memory.
They have the ring of earlier credal formulae, and may already have been familiar to his readers as such; but from his
point of view they would thereby be all the more effective as
safeguards against dangerously new and different ideas.

The deputation from the city of Tralles, headed by their
bishop, also reported congregational conflict over the reality
of Jesus' physical sufferings. Again, Ignatius advises them not
even to listen to such talk. The whole point of his own im-
pending death would be lost, he believes, if Jesus Christ had
not suffered a real death:

Be deaf, then, to any talk that ignores Jesus Christ, of David's
lineage, of Mary; who was really born, ate, and drank; was really
persecuted under Pontius Pilate; was really crucified and died, in
the sight of heaven and earth and the underworld. He was really
raised from the dead. . . . And if, as some atheists (I mean un-
believers) say, his suffering was a sham (it's really *they* who are a
sham!) why, then, am I a prisoner? Why do I want to fight with
wild beasts? In that case I shall die to no purpose.[7]

When his party stopped in Smyrna, Ignatius met the
effects of docetist teaching at first hand. In the later letter to
that city, he adds detail to detail, to underline Jesus' historical reality: ". . . . on the human side he was actually
sprung from David's line . . . actually born of a virgin,

baptized by John . . . and actually crucified for us in the flesh, under Pontius Pilate and Herod the Tetrarch." [8] Correct thinking on this subject is essential, Ignatius argues, because of its practical consequences. If one denies the physical reality of Jesus Christ, one is also likely to deny the need for physical expression of Christian love; and for the same reason, one attaches little importance to the material forms of Christian worship:

Pay close attention to those who have wrong notions about the grace of Jesus Christ, which has come to us, and note how at variance they are with God's mind. They care nothing about love; they have no concern for widows or orphans, for the oppressed, for those in prison or released, for the hungry or the thirsty. They hold aloof from the Eucharist and from services of prayer, because they refuse to admit that the Eucharist is the flesh of our Saviour Jesus Christ. . . .[9]

According to Ignatius of Antioch, whom later Christians counted among those writers known as the "Apostolic Fathers," the value of the material world is assured by the humanity of Jesus Christ. Denying his real participation in its sufferings leads to indifference about the physical needs and sufferings of others.

Seventy years after Ignatius, a theologian in Western Europe, Irenaeus, Bishop of Lyons, launched a more direct attack upon the explicit gnostic position. He undertook "The Refutation and Overthrow of the Knowledge Falsely So Called." Tradition knows his major work more simply, but less accurately, as *Against Heresies*. In recent years there has been a considerable revival of theological interest in Irenaeus, but he made his permanent contribution to Christian thought by concentrating on the problems of his own diocese.[10] He complained that gnostic teachers right in his own district of the Rhone were attracting well-bred and elegantly attired

Christian matrons with hocus-pocus.[11] Because the credulity
and emotionalism of such women created a serious pastoral
situation, the bishop attempted both an exposé of their false
superstitions and, in design, a clear exposition of the Christian
counterview.

IRENAEUS' DEFENSE OF CREATION

In the process, Irenaeus develops the kind of argument
Ignatius had merely suggested, by relating the Incarnation
to the Eucharist. He adds a major theme which Ignatius did
not emphasize, a defense of creation itself. Given their matter-
spirit dualism, the gnostics not only had difficulty accepting
a real Incarnation; they also found it impossible to believe
the biblical doctrine that God looked on his creation and
found it very good. Irenaeus ridicules the self-contradiction
of calling oneself a Christian, and participating in Christian
worship, while embracing gnostic ideas about the origin of
the universe. The bread and wine offered in the Eucharist
are mere insults if they are not the fruits of a good earth:

Those, again, who maintain that the things around us originated
from apostasy, ignorance, and passion, do while offering unto
Him the fruits of ignorance, passion, and apostasy, sin against
the Father, rather subjecting Him to insult than giving Him
thanks. But how can they be consistent with themselves [when
they say] that the bread over which thanks has been given is the
body of their Lord, and the cup His blood, if they do not call
Himself the Son of the Creator of the world, that is, His word
through whom the wood fructifies and the fountains gush forth,
and the earth gives forth "first the blade, then the ear, then the
full corn in the ear. . . ." Let them, therefore, either alter their
opinion, or cease from offering the things just mentioned. But
our opinion is in accordance with the Eucharist, and the Eucharist in turn establishes our opinion. For we offer to Him, His

own, announcing consistently the fellowship and union of the flesh and spirit.[12]

Irenaeus wants consistency between Christian thinking and Christian behavior. The consistent position, as he sees it, is one which holds "the fellowship and union of the flesh and spirit." Central to the theological position developed in his five books against heresies, is a sacramental view which affirms and unites, rather than separates, what he calls "the two realities, earthly and heavenly." Insistence on the ultimate value of the created world even leads the Gallican bishop, with remarkable self-consistency, to some bizarre speculations at the end of his work about the details of nature as it will be in the coming age of the kingdom. Taking an Isaiah prophecy literally, he envisions the lion eating straw and marvels at the implied fertility of the earth then. "For if such an animal as the lion feeds on straw, what kind of grain must it be whose very straw is suitable food for lions?" Neither the substance nor the essence of the created order will vanish away, as Irenaeus views the future, for "since men are real, they must have a real existence." [13]

Speculations about the future are relatively rare in the theological writings we have from the second century, however. The Christian community was more concerned to deal with the problems of its own present. Gnosticism, in its many forms and guises, was a very real threat to the young Church, and its success in winning the minds of men undoubtedly hastened the growth of an ordered institutional life among Christians. By the end of Irenaeus' life, the Church had developed or strengthened four bulwarks against attack, four forms of self-identification and self-preservation, which play a decisive role in the subsequent growth of Christian thought. The office of bishop as guardian of the faith, the liturgy for ordered worship, and the canon of scripture all saw new definition in the years of battle against gnosticism. So, too, did a formal Christian creed. Between Ignatius' almost certain slaughter in the Roman Coliseum and Irenaeus' recorded visit to Rome in A.D. 177, some sixty years later, the direct ancestor of that statement of faith known as the Apostles' Creed came into being.

One of the false teachers whom Irenaeus attacked in his "Refutation and Overthrow of the Knowledge Falsely So Called" was a man by the name of Marcion. Although originally from Pontus near the Black Sea, Marcion was exceedingly popular in Rome in the mid-century. He is said to have won over half of the Christians in the capital city of the Empire to his teaching. Scholars disagree as to whether Marcion may properly be classed as a gnostic; there is even more serious debate about the extent of his influence on the Apostles' Creed. We do not have enough evidence to decide these historical questions with finality. Both question marks admitted, Marcion nevertheless taught a religious dualism limiting the religiously significant to a spiritual realm. And deliberately or not, the Old Roman Symbol from which the Apostles' Creed developed is in fact a repudiation of this kind of thinking, in the name of the Christian revelation.

Marcion's popularity as a religious teacher was not limited to Rome. A contemporary complained that he had "made many in every race of men to blaspheme." [14] He considered himself a Christian; but, sharing St. Paul's conviction that Christ brought an entirely new life to men, he could see no connection between Christianity and Judaism. One of his favorite scriptural texts seems to have been Luke 5:37, "No one puts new wine into old wineskins." The God of the Old Testament, the Creator God, and the God revealed in Christ, he concluded, were two different gods. The Creator of the world was real, but inferior to "the Father who is above the God that formed the world." [15] Jesus was from the latter God, the God of love.

Marcion evidently held originally that the Creator God

was responsible for both matter and spirit, but the ethics of his group argue a developed antithesis between them. Marcionites were rigorous ascetics. They were to eat no meat and drink no wine, even in their Eucharist. They were forbidden to have sexual intercourse.

Marcion's ideas must be reconstructed from the writings of his opponents, men like Irenaeus, Justin Martyr, and especially Tertullian, who wrote a lengthy work against him. But these sources all support the five-point summary of his teaching drawn by A. C. McGiffert:

1. That the God of Christians is not the creator and ruler of the universe, but another being who was entirely unknown until revealed by Jesus Christ.

2. That Jesus Christ is the son of the latter being.

3. That God, the Father of Jesus Christ, is a being of pure love and mercy, and will judge no one.

4. That Christ's life was that of a spirit only, his bodily form only appearance.

5. That the flesh of men does not rise again.[16]

THE CHURCH'S CREDAL AFFIRMATION

In a lecture first delivered at the Harvard Summer School of Theology back in 1899, Professor McGiffert argued forcefully that these teachings are consciously denied in the creed which Christians in Rome began to use shortly after Marcion's career there. Recent studies support a more positive, catechetical motive behind the expansion of the simple baptismal formula.[17] Without accepting the thesis that the creed was developed chiefly or deliberately as anti-Marcionite propaganda, however, one may well observe that what the Church did choose to affirm in the earliest known form of the Apostles' Creed expressly rules out each of these Marcionite doctrines:

I believe in God *almighty*.
And in Christ Jesus, *his* only son, our Lord
Who was *born* of the Holy Spirit and the Virgin Mary
Who was *crucified* under Pontius Pilate and was *buried*.
And the third day rose from the *dead*.
Who ascended into heaven
And sitteth on the right hand of the Father
Whence he cometh to *judge* the living and the dead.
And in the Holy Ghost
The holy church
The remission of sins
The resurrection of the *flesh*
The life everlasting.[18]

In another age than our own, Christians were deeply troubled by the relationship between matter and spirit. In the process of combating the metaphysical, ethical, and religious dualisms of the day, they came to reaffirm certain basic ideas: that the one God created heaven and earth, matter and spirit, body and soul; that Jesus Christ, his Son, was truly born, truly suffered, truly died, with no sham involved; that the material world is therefore, as it were, doubly important—a good creation re-created. If the Christian believes this, they said, he can use and offer the material of creation, bread and wine, money and sex, with true thanksgiving. If he shares this view, he has sufficient motive to care realistically for the well-being of his neighbor in embodied expression of Christian love. Refusing the easy dichotomies of gnostic spiritualism, they came, in short, to insist that matter is the necessary medium of the Spirit. The second-century theologians would agree with Archbishop Temple's remark that Christianity is the most avowedly materialist of all the great religions.[19]

CHAPTER 7

The Deity of Christ

Not very many years ago churchgoers commonly thought of Jesus as a poor man who made good. Protestant Christianity, particularly in America, was convinced that Jesus of Nazareth was a great success. The Christianity of Main Street cherished a log cabin–to–White House story:

However humble his origins, Jesus lived an exemplary life—such an exemplary life that he won friends and influenced people not only in Palestine but around the world; not only in the first century but forever after. He taught men to love their neighbors as themselves, and he practiced what he preached. Therefore his Heavenly Father rewarded him with eternal life. If we truly follow his teaching, we too will not really die.[1]

This popular version of the Christian story ignored the fact that, by every human standard, Jesus was not a success at all. Quite the contrary. According to the record, he was gradually abandoned by one friend after another, until he was left alone—to die by torture, mocked by a hostile crowd. Hardly the kind of success story that excites enthusiasm to go and do likewise. But the trouble with this version of Christianity was not merely its lack of candor. It represented such a complete reversal of Christian thought that it could not properly be called Christian at all. Classical Christianity through the centuries had told a diametrically different story, not the story of a man promoted from a log cabin to the White House, but rather the story of a King's son voluntarily moving from a palace to live in the slums. And therein lay the problem.

Who Is Jesus?

Many forces combined to overturn the classic story, but one of the strongest was philosophical. The claims of Christian orthodoxy were a stumbling block to post-Kantian reason. In the heyday of Protestant liberalism, students spent hours in earnest discussion of "the divinity of Christ." They agreed that intelligent men and women could have vast admiration for the person of Jesus. He might even have been the greatest human being in recorded history, although the Buddha was undoubtedly a close second. But what did it mean to say also that he was God? If Jesus was really God, who was running the universe while he was walking around in Galilee? Who controlled reality while he lay wrapped in swaddling clothes or hung dying on the cross?

Or again, if instead of saying that Jesus was God, one said that he was the Son of God, what did this mean? In what sense could a person make such an affirmation? To call him the Son of God might be all right provided one understood that title to mean a status equally open to all men who achieve the same fulness of life. After all, if God is a Heavenly Father, then we are all sons of God. But to take this statement seriously, making a claim about a unique status in being, must mean that there are really two gods, must it not? One the Father and the other the Son.

Failure to find answers to such fumbling questions led some people into the Unitarian Church, which makes no paradoxical claims about the One God being both Father and Son. It merely led others, who could no longer think honestly about Jesus Christ as either God or Son of God, out of the churches which taught this incomprehensible doctrine. Some who remained found their churches no longer saying much about it.

I have been speaking in the past tense, because in the last twenty-five years the man left in the pew has become a great deal more sophisticated in his understanding of the Christian faith. A generation of preachers has proclaimed again the old good news that in Christ God was reconciling the world unto himself. It is no longer even necessary to label these preachers "neo-orthodox." And the result may well be that the current generation of churchmen is in far greater danger of thinking of the Christ as not fully human, of introducing a new docetism such as the last chapter described. But are the questions about the deity of Christ really dead questions, or have they just gone underground? Do Christians know what they mean, and mean what they say, when they recite the familiar words:

. . . and in one Lord, Jesus Christ, the only-begotten Son of God; Begotten, not made; Being of one substance with the Father; By whom all things were made . . . ?

Do such statements have any cognitive value today?

Our age is still an age in search of a Christian philosophy. So was the age which formulated the second major creed of Christendom and therefore these phrases, which slide so easily from our lips in worship but stumble before the bar of intellect. When the Council of Nicea originally accepted them in A.D. 325, the phrases were already the subject of much bitter debate. They remained the center of controversy for the better part of the fourth century. Some of the ablest men of the Church devoted their whole careers to explaining and defending the thesis that the Son was of one substance with the Father (even though such defense sometimes brought political exile). With equal fervor, and with equally serious results, other able men spent their lives denying the thesis. Imperial Rome had no doubt that ideas have consequences.

This particular intellectual battle was part of a larger problem in the Christian Church in the fourth century. For the first time, the Church was forced to come to terms with culture. Hitherto it had been largely preoccupied with its own internal problems, and with preserving its own life against a series of attempts either to render it impotent or to stamp it out entirely. By and large, therefore, third-century Christians contented themselves with one of two attitudes toward the larger culture in which they were a minority group. Men like the sharp-witted and sharp-tongued Tertullian saw nothing but conflict between the Church and the world. His famous question, "What has Athens to do with Jerusalem?" epitomizes the radical opposition many believers thought must inevitably exist between Christian faith and the whole cultural heritage of classical civilization. At the opposite pole, hospitable minds like that of Clement of Alexandria welcomed all of the best thought of past or present, often with uncritical enthusiasm. Clement and others of this stripe could think of Plato and Christ walking together on the path to true philosophy. Both schools of thought accepted and used of Christ the scriptural language of Son and Word, but as yet there had been no urgent need to think through and defend publicly its precise philosophical and theological implications.

After Constantine became sole emperor in 311, however, and proceeded first to end persecution of the Church and then to promote it to new respectability, churchmen faced a new intellectual task. Their problem, as Charles Norris Cochrane summarizes it, was to formulate their belief in terms faithful to scripture and at the same time comprehensible to the contemporary mind. With the Emperor calling on the Church to provide a remedy for the ills of an expiring world, the Church now had "to work out the elements of a philosophy in keeping with its own distinctive first principles." [2]

It was not permitted leisure for the job. When a theological quarrel shook the new peace of the Church, Constantine took action. His biographer Eusebius tells us that "he fulminated like a powerful herald of God against intestine strife within the Church as more dangerous than any kind of war or conflict." [3] He did not understand the issues in the quarrel, but he summoned a general council to his imperial palace at Nicea to settle them. The main issue on the council agenda concerned the deity of Christ.

THE ARIAN CONTROVERSY

The uproar had started some eight years earlier in the university city of Alexandria, when a priest named Arius accused his bishop of overstressing the unity of God. Like so many of the men later defined as heretics, Arius is a cloudy figure. Since most of the information about him comes from his opponents, caution is indicated. Yet there is some historical evidence to support a picture of Arius as the prototype of a popular university pastor—personally ambitious, proud of his following of devoted students and suburban matrons, ready to use the latest techniques of public relations to communicate the Gospel. Arius may even have encouraged his followers to turn out catchy jingles setting his doctrines to popular, bawdy tunes for barber shop consumption:

> If you want the Logos-doctrine, I can serve it
> hot and hot—

God begat him and before He was begotten,
He was not.[4]

Theology was evidently as much a matter of public interest
in Alexandria in those days as it was sixty years later in Constantinople, when Gregory of Nazianzus worried because silly
talk about theology at every dinner party and in all the
women's apartments was making trivial the great mystery of
the Faith.[5]

Stronger historical evidence allows a reconstruction of
Arius' teaching. Alarmed because he thought that his bishop
was reducing the Son of God to a mere power or function of
the Father, Arius started preaching about the difference between Father and Son. To do so, he invoked the neo-Platonic
idea of a monad beyond knowledge and beyond existence,
the one source of all things whatsoever. This God was therefore the source of the Word, or Logos. As Arius interpreted
the Christian proclamation, the Logos of God was himself a
creature, different in eternity and in essence from God the
Father. True, he is to be thought of as different from all other
creatures also—as having his being "before times and before
ages," as divine, unique, and unchangeable.[6] Nevertheless,
"there was when he was not." Arius, as an ancient church
historian observed, was "a man not lacking in dialectic," [7]
and his arguments are carefully stated; but in effect he conceived of the Word as a kind of demigod. His followers were
happy to borrow a phrase from an earlier age, less troubled
with exact expression, to call the Logos "a second god." Such,
at any rate, is the accusation made against them.

To Alexander, Bishop of Alexandria, and to the Egyptian Synod which he called to deal with the matter, this teaching seemed to provide ample grounds for excommunicating
Arius. To Eusebius, Bishop of Caesarea and an old school
friend of Arius', on the other hand, it sounded like the theology they had both learned from their former teacher, Lu-

cian of Antioch. Regional loyalty and ecclesiastical jealousy soon entered to spread the fight beyond the diocese and to complicate the theological issues at Nicea. Constantine himself presided over that Council, a symbol of the new reconciliation between Church and state. The majority of the bishops present determined to adopt a statement of Christian faith which would decisively exclude an Arian reading. Although some were reluctant to introduce non-scriptural language for the purpose, only a technical philosophical term would do the trick. Accordingly, the assembled fathers proposed to say that the Son of God was *homoousios* with the Father.

Three observations about this proposal are in order. In the first place, abstract speculative thought always flourished in Hellenistic culture. Barber shops and boudoirs buzzed with theological controversy in the fourth century, because the people, in Alexandria or in Constantinople, enjoyed it. Roman citizens they might now be, but in spirit their culture was still the grandchild of Alexander the Great, pupil of Aristotle. Mental exercise was a favorite sport, indoors and out.

Probably because they enjoyed ideas, they had developed, in the second place, a vocabulary adequate to their mental agility. They had words to make it possible to say just what they meant. The Greek-speaking Eastern Empire thus had a great advantage over their Western brethren, where Latin had finally come to be used for intellectual activity as well as for ordinary affairs. The Eastern theologians, for example, had two terms for *being*. The more general was *ousia*, which the Latins translated as *substantia*, literally meaning "to stand under." Unfortunately, this is also the literal meaning of the other Greek word for being, individuated being, or *hypostasis*, so that when this word had also to be translated into Latin, that language had no proper equivalent left. The word they chose was *persona*. Rendered yet again into English, *ousia* and *hypostasis* thus become *substance* and *person,* which in modern ears inevitably connote solidity and personality—ideas which are about as remote as possible from what the fourth century was talking about.

What they were talking about throughout this whole controversy, before, during, and after the Nicene Council, was the nature of ultimate being. This is the third thing to observe. The discussion is all about the being of God, as he was in the beginning, is now, and ever shall be. And in order to understand this, one should almost try for the moment to forget all about any incarnation. The Son and the Logos of the Arian controversy (to exaggerate absurdly) have almost nothing to do with Jesus of Nazareth.

With this in mind, let us return to the Council. By saying that "there was when he was not," the Arians made the Son, or Logos, less than ultimate being. The Council now entertained the motion that the term *homoousios* be used, to make it quite clear that the Logos of scripture was essentially one with God, that the Son of scripture was *being* of one substance with the Father. The term was accepted. It became part of the credal statement adopted by Nicea, and was included in the expanded creed later adopted by the Council of Constantinople (the creed which is confusingly known by Christians today as the Nicene Creed). By accepting it, the bishops did not end the dispute Constantine had intended to stifle. The word *homoousios* itself became a battle cry of the Arian controversy, which now began in earnest. By altering it one iota, one could make it mean merely "like" in substance, rather than identical; and this proposal is the subject of another chapter in the history of the long debate. To modern believers, reading this history for the first time, the Nicene controversy can easily sound like a petty semantic squabble. To the participants it was literally a matter of life and death. One of the historians best qualified to judge the implications of the quarrel contends that "for those who believe that what men do has a direct relationship to what they think and what they want, it is impossible to avoid the issues raised at that time." [8]

THE ATHANASIAN DEFENSE

The man who realized the seriousness of the issue more than anyone else, who became the great defender of the Nicene faith, was present at Nicea only as secretary to his bishop, Alexander. This man was Athanasius. Probably still a deacon in 325, he could not have taken any important role in the deliberations of the Council, but literary license permits anachronism. To dramatize the implications of the Arian use of words, Dorothy Sayers makes Athanasius say to the Emperor:

Suppose there is a grammarian in your empire who says: "I am very willing, like everybody else, to call Constantine *Augustus*—for that word need after all mean only *dignified, noble,* or the like, and such he undoubtedly is. But that Constantine is our rightful emperor I do not and will not admit. Therefore, when I call him *Augustus* it is with the mental reservation that I understand the word in my own way and not the other, and this is the meaning that I shall teach to everyone who hears me lecture." Supposing this were to come to your august ears. . . .

At which point Constantine interrupts to say, "I should have him arrested on the spot." [9]

Athanasius is a giant in the history of Christian thought. Three years after attending the Council of Nicea, he succeeded to the See of Alexandria; he was still bishop at his death in 373, having survived five periods of banishment for stubbornly refusing to trim his principles to fit changing imperial policy in the fight over Arianism. When he would not agree to restore an apparently repentant Arius to his former place among the clergy of Alexandria, he was exiled

to Gaul for two years. On another occasion, under another
emperor, he took refuge among the desert monks in Egypt.
His admiration for the ascetic life of these earliest monastics
is expressed in one of his best-known writings, a life of An-
thony the hermit saint, whom he claims to have known from
his youth. Most of Athanasius' writings, however, are direct
attacks on the Arian position or direct defense of the Nicene
alternative. At times Athanasius felt himself to be alone
against the world; but he could not relinquish his stand without relinquishing, he believed, man's only chance for salvation.

When he came to the end of his forty-five-year episcopate,
Athanasius had not completely triumphed. Arian Christianity
had won the allegiance of many in the Roman Empire, and
Arian missionaries had carried their faith to the Teutonic
tribes of Western Europe with such success that the barbarian
invaders of Rome in the fifth and sixth centuries were Arian
Christians. But for catholic Christianity, Athanasius and his
followers had preserved the Nicene faith that Father and Son
are one in being. Eight years after his death the Eastern
bishops, meeting in council at Constantinople, summed up
their long struggle over the nature of the one God in these
words:

For whether we endured persecutions or afflictions, or imperial
threats or the cruelties of governors, or any other trial from the
heretics, we withstood all for the sake of the gospel faith as au-
thenticated by the 318 Fathers at Nicaea in Bithynia.[10]

The gospel faith, the good news, as Athanasius understood it, was news of salvation. It depended on a real union
between God and man, between the Creator and his creature.
This union, and this alone, could confer on sinful man the
gift of immortality. This salvation from death was wrought by
the incarnation of the Word of God. But, given the presup-

positions with which Athanasius was working, salvation was literally impossible in Arian terms. Arius was trying to bridge an infinite gap with a finite being.

Athanasius thought of God as the ground and source of being. As he explained in his early work refuting paganism, "God is not nature, all the constituents of which are mutually interdependent. Nor is He the totality of its parts; for He is not compounded of parts on which He depends, but is Himself the source of existence to all." [11] Along with this denial of pantheism goes denial of the pagan idea that God used some pre-existent matter to put together the universe. Creation is *ex nihilo*, out of nothing. "God creates by calling the non-existent into being." [12] For Athanasius, Christian thinking begins with God the Creator.

All creatures, on the other hand, have a beginning; and accordingly all creatures must have an end. Formerly non-existent, man is by definition a creature. Since he derives his being from God, who alone *is*, it follows that without God he would be turned back to what is not. In other words, he would be disintegrated. "For man is by nature mortal, in as much as he is made out of what is not." [13] With such an absolute antithesis between what is and what is not, between being and non-being, there is only one possible way for death to be overcome.

If, as Arius said, the Word had a beginning, he was a creature and would therefore necessarily have an end also. But if he is God, it is impossible for him to suffer death. At the outset of his treatise on the Incarnation, Athanasius identifies the Logos with God in the sharpest possible terms:

It is, then, proper for us to begin the treatment of this subject by speaking of the creation of the universe, and of God its Artificer, that so it may be duly perceived that the renewal of creation has been the work of the selfsame Word that made it at the beginning.[14]

He supports this by quoting St. John's "all things were made through him, and without him was not anything made."

To effect salvation, the Creator, then, "takes to himself a body capable of death, that it, by partaking of the Word who is above all . . . might, because of the Word which was come to dwell in it, remain incorruptible, and that thenceforth corruption might be stayed from all by the grace of the resurrection." [15] The body of Jesus Christ was human; it died, as Athanasius says, "conformably to its peers." But by virtue of its union with the Word, it was no longer subject to the fate of non-being. The God-Man conquered death. Or, as he later put it with far greater simplicity, "He was made man that we might be made God." [16]

Critics of Athanasius through the centuries have charged that this last statement is just the old, well-worn Greek idea of apotheosis. They are wrong. Literally, it reads, "He was humanized that we might be deified." [17] In all essential respects, as Cochrane insists, it represents a real change from classical ways of thought. To the Greek mind, deification was possible only for the hero or the superman. To the Christian, it was now thought possible for everyman—as a gift from God. In developing this new idea, Athanasius often quoted three New Testament texts: John 1:12, "to all who received him . . . he gave power to become children of God"; I Cor. 3:16, "Do you not know that you are God's temple and that God's Spirit dwells in you?"; II Peter 1:4, "that you may become partakers of the divine nature." He was trying to be a responsible biblical theologian and yet make the Christian faith comprehensible to educated men of his day. As he saw it, Christian faith offered life to dying men, and that was possible only if the incarnate Word was *homoousios* with the Father.

CHAPTER 8

The Seriousness
of Sin

Shortly before midnight on May 31, 1962, Adolf Eichmann was hanged. He had been found guilty of infamous crimes, committed under the Nazi regime against the Jewish people. In spite of his claims that he was only obeying orders, that he was the victim of the power structure, he was judged responsible. He was executed. Reporting on Eichmann's dramatic trial before the eyes of the world, Hannah Arendt documents "the totality of the moral collapse the Nazis caused in respectable European society—not only in Germany but in almost all countries, not only among the persecutors but also among the victims." [1] The prosecution was totally unable to prove that Eichmann had been a sadist or any other kind of a monster. "The trouble with Eichmann was precisely that so many were like him, and that the many were neither perverted nor sadistic, that they were, and still are, terribly and terrifyingly normal." [2]

THE BANALITY OF SIN IN SOCIETY

Up to the end, Eichmann believed fervently in "good society," according to Miss Arendt—and in success, the chief standard of that good society as he knew it. The Nazis did not succeed. As a result of their failure, Eichmann and other war criminals were declared guilty. But, Miss Arendt asks, "Would any one of them have suffered from a guilty conscience if they had won?" [3]

The subtitle of this controversial book, on an even more controversial legal case, is "A Report on the Banality of Evil." Millions of human beings were deliberately exterminated in the middle of the twentieth century, it suggests, not because of a few Eichmanns, but because most of us are what we are —no better and no worse. It suggests that for the same reason thousands of people starve each year, while other thousands buy Metrecal. That hundreds of competent men and women with one color of skin are jobless, while hundreds with a different skin pigmentation figure out ways to cut their income tax. Commonplace, yes. But how is one to account for such banality? And what is one to do about it?

One very attractive approach to these major questions speaks of human freedom and human responsibility. In this view, Eichmann would be a magnificent symbol of our common human tendency to escape from freedom, to retreat into some authoritarian religion or totalitarian government where buck-passing techniques come ready-made. There are certain dichotomies of human existence, it is argued, which man must learn to accept. He can do nothing about the fact that he is going to die, nor about the fact that his life will be too short for him to realize all his goals and potentialities. By nature he is both an individual and a member of a community, and he must learn to live with the tensions resulting from being at once related and alone.

On the other hand, there are many dichotomies in life which are merely the product of human history, and which are open to change through human action. We may not yet know how to share equitably the produce of the land, for example, but there is no ultimate reason why we cannot learn to do so. Instead of appeasing his mind with soothing ideologies emphasizing either individual human weakness or social forces over which he has no control, man should stand on his hind legs and act the man. He should have confidence in human reason and faith in human capacity gradually to solve the complex social problems of the world.[4]

Humanists, theist and atheist alike, share this general attitude toward the misery of mankind. With many among them who call themselves Christians, the former would probably be willing to use the word *sin* in their diagnosis of social evils, and for that failure of nerve which holds back so many men from direct attack upon them. They would probably add "with the help of God" to the suggested remedy. The latter feel that they have outgrown the orthodoxy which talks of God and sin. Indeed, to many humanists the concepts of sin, and particularly of original sin, are partly responsible for the ills of mankind. As everyone knows, an inferiority complex or neurotic guilt can cause all sorts of aberrations in human behavior. Such complexes not only help explain but can in fact produce both Hitlers and Eichmanns. Whether from theist or non-theist, however, the humanist prescription is similar. Man is a responsible moral being. Let him act more responsibly to produce the social environment in which all men can grow into free, whole, loving beings.

In a very effective cartoon published not long ago, a psychiatrist announced to his patient stretched on his couch, "Mr. Jones, you don't have an inferiority complex. You *are* inferior." The orthodox Christian must answer something very much like this to the attractive, reasonable voice of humanism. He finds the humanist diagnosis and the humanist

remedy inadequate, because he believes that the disease of
mankind is too serious to respond just to moral imperatives.
He acknowledges, rather, a separation from the source of the
power of Good. And so, lamenting its sin, the Christian
Church continues to pray, "Almighty God, who seest that we
have no power of ourselves to help ourselves. . . ." Or again,
"because, through the weakness of our mortal nature, we can
do no good thing without thee, grant us the help of thy
grace. . . ." Or yet again,

O Lord, we beseech thee favourably to hear the prayers of thy
people; that we, who are justly punished for our offences, may be
mercifully delivered by thy goodness, for the glory of thy Name,
through Jesus Christ our Saviour. . . .[5]

All three of these prayers go back to another period of
crisis in Western civilization, when perceptive spirits were
writing of widespread moral collapse. They date from the
fifth and sixth centuries, when the powers and problems of
human nature were similarly at the center of religious debate.
Fifth-century Romans knew that they were living in an age
of the setting sun. They saw the bankruptcy of their own
society almost as clearly as they saw the empire shrinking
before the barbarian invaders. From that other decadent culture, Jerome speaks to those who listened to the testimony
of the Eichmann trial: "The mind shudders when dwelling
on the ruin of our day. . . . On every side sorrow, on every
side lamentation, everywhere the image of death." [6] From that
other age of hedonism, those who reflect on the banality of
evil can hear also the voices of Pelagius and Augustine, raised
in a third great debate of Christian history.

EMPHASIS ON HUMAN RESPONSIBILITY

Pelagius, tradition tells us, was a British monk, lately
come to the metropolis of the world. Even if more accurate

historians now believe that he had lived there a long time, one still cannot resist the impression that his shocked reaction to Roman immorality was partly the response of any country man to the life of a big city. Centuries before him, Amos, the herdsman from Tekoa, had experienced it in Bethel; he proclaimed God's judgment on Israel. Centuries later, a Broadway ingenue experienced it in New York; she lamented ever having left Ohio. In Rome at the beginning of the fifth century, Pelagius reacted by preaching moral rearmament.

According to the charges later made against him, Pelagius was convinced that God's law can and must be obeyed. Being just, God would not command man to do the impossible. Since he has given man a moral law, he must also have given him the capacity to fulfill it. Apparently Pelagius found the Christians in Rome using the doctrine of original sin as an excuse for their own moral laxity. They could not really help sinning, they said; it was all Adam's fault. Incensed at this blatant rationalization, Pelagius taught that Adam's sin injured no one but himself. Each man is fully responsible for his own actions. It is true that he may be hampered by the weight of his own bad habits, and by the bad example of others; but in Jesus Christ he has been given a good example. Let him try a little harder to follow it. Finally Pelagius was led by the logic of his own position to deny the universal need for baptism. Since an infant does not inherit the guilt of Adam's sin, he is not condemned simply because this guilt has not been washed away.

Controversy undoubtedly lends clarity to a man's thinking. When Pelagius started preaching in Rome, he may not have given such unqualified support to the thesis, "if I ought, I can." But after Pelagius had visited Africa in 410, this is what Augustine, Bishop of Hippo, began fighting against. It was a long fight. The final round—if, indeed, it can be said ever to have ended—did not come until a century after Augustine's death, when in 529 the Council of Orange condemned a position known by then as semi-Pelagianism. Before his death, Augustine himself wrote fifteen polemic works against Pelagian teaching. In them he reaffirmed social responsibility for sin. He insisted that all men are infected with the sin of Adam, and that all need baptism to remove the effects of this sin. Most of all, he insisted that man can do nothing by himself to lead the kind of life he knows he ought to.

AUGUSTINE'S ASSERTION: THE ABSOLUTE NECESSITY OF GRACE

To understand the depth of Augustine's resistance to Pelagian ideas, and the breadth of his positive thinking in opposition, one must look beyond the works classified as anti-Pelagian. Augustine's vehement rejection of this sturdy Christian moralism remains incomprehensible apart from his own religious experience. Some of his statements in the last weary years of the struggle remain distorted until they are seen in the perspective of other statements made on other battle fronts. But it is not easy to see Augustine whole. It would not be easy in the case of any man who wrote ninety-seven books in the course of a thirty-four-year episcopate.

Pelagius saw no reason why a man could not do what he knew full well he ought to do. Augustine was convinced by his own experience that things are not that simple. The sins of his youth are undoubtedly somewhat exaggerated in his *Confessions* (as they certainly are by people today who have heard the title but never read the book), but some exaggeration was inevitable for this twice-born man. From the haven of Christian faith, he remembered a wild sea; from the new-found sunlight, a mighty storm.

In search of meaning and direction for his life, the young intellectual had worked his way successively through most of the philosophies known to his generation. He started out on the disinterested quest for truth which Cicero had advocated.

Then for eight years, until he was disappointed by the mentality of its most famous preacher, he embraced the current form of gnosticism, an eclectic religion known as Manicheanism. Academic skepticism and neo-Platonism each attracted him for a short time thereafter. By the time the young professor of rhetoric went to Milan to listen to Bishop Ambrose, an acknowledged master of Augustine's own subject, he had tried them all without finding either happiness or the will power for the good life which he sought.

The controversy in his heart of "self against self" [7] ended one day in a country-house garden when he read St. Paul's words, "Not in rioting and drunkenness, not in chambering and wantonness, not in strife and envying: but put ye on the Lord Jesus Christ. . . ." After that, Augustine tells us, "by a light as it were of serenity infused into my heart, all the darkness of doubt vanished away." [8] But that new faith still did not allow Augustine to be at ease about his past sins. Not until he and his son were baptized by Ambrose on Easter, 387, can he report that "anxiety for our past life vanished from us." [9]

Born anew in this experience of God's forgiving love, Augustine, Christian, became in the Church the great doctor of grace. He shared fully Pelagius' concern for individual moral responsibility. He believed that a Christian can only say, "I am responsible; I am guilty." But at the same time, he was fully convinced that man cannot reform himself. He cannot just decide to try harder. The only effective initiative and power is the grace of God, the divine love in action. In all his teaching, the root problem is therefore this existential problem of sin and grace. Only secondarily is it translated into more abstract terms, into the intellectual problem of free will *versus* determinism. With many variations in his many writings, Augustine works out his positive theological answer to the dilemma of experience which must ascribe all good to God alone and all sin to man alone.

Man, as Augustine understands him, is by nature good. All being is good, because it comes from God, the source of being who supremely *is* and who is supremely good. "A man," Augustine says in so many words, "is a good thing because he is a being." [10] Using ideas encountered in neo-Platonic philosophy, Augustine defines evil as the absence or privation of the good. A disease or wound in the body of an animal, he argues, is nothing but the absence of health. By the same token, what we call vices "are nothing but privations of natural good." [11] In so far as they exist, things are good. The only cause of evil is a falling away from the good. By definition, such a falling away involves an actual loss of being.

Man was created as a rational being, with freedom to direct his love toward the good. Misusing his freedom, he misdirected his love. He turned away from the good, the center, the real. He thus suffered a genuine loss of being, a change in human nature, such that he is no longer capable of that freedom or that love for which he was created. What he needs is a gift of new being, and this can come only from God. For Augustine, then, Jesus is more than a good example. God's redemptive act in Christ is precisely that needed restitution of full personal existence. God offers man a restoration of being, a new manhood, because without it, it is impossible for him to be himself and hence to will and to do the good. "We are now," Augustine writes, "newly created in Christ." [12]

In his treatise "The Spirit and the Letter," addressed to the imperial legate Marcellinus, who had written Augustine asking for fuller explanation of some statements made in earlier writings against the Pelagians, Augustine expounds this theme of grace most clearly. As the basis of his work, he chooses St. Paul's letter to the Romans. Augustine interprets the text of Second Corinthians 3:6, "the letter killeth, but the Spirit giveth life," in the light of Paul's whole argument in that Romans letter, and particularly in the light of the complementary text from chapter 5, that now "God's love has been poured into our hearts through the Holy Spirit which has been given to us."

No matter what the Pelagians say, without the help of God the human will does not have the power either to achieve perfect righteousness or to advance steadily toward it. In addition to being taught how he *ought* to live, man needs—and he is given—the Holy Spirit, "the Spirit of grace," to enable him to delight in doing so. Augustine believes, with Paul, that this great gift comes to man through faith in Jesus Christ, whose death and resurrection meant the destruction of sin and the renewal of righteousness. He quotes Paul's words: "Know ye not, that so many of us as were baptized in Christ Jesus were baptized into his death. Therefore we are buried with him by baptism into death, that like as Christ rose from the dead through the glory of the Father, even so we also should walk in newness of life." From this gift, which is his here and now, "there arises in his soul the delight in and the love of God, the supreme and changeless Good," so that "he may be fired in heart to cleave to his Creator, kindled in mind to come within the shining of the true light; and thus receive from the source of his being the only real well-being." [13]

As long as man trusts in self and makes "the self the spring of its own life" (which is the sin of pride), he cannot have "the righteousness which is good life." [14] If he trusts in Christ, he receives healing from the very fountain of life. Grace is given him, "a mending of nature," which restores the will, so that the restored will may fulfill the law. All men must come by faith "to know that any good in their life is theirs by the grace of God, and that their perfecting in the love of righteousness can come about in no other way." [15] "By the faith of Jesus Christ—the faith, that is, which Christ has conferred upon us," Augustine explains, "we believe that from God is given to us and will be given yet more fully the life of righteousness. Wherefore . . . we give him thanks." [16] Thanksgiving is in order because, as he understands it, there can be no better good, no happier happiness than this: "life for God, life from God, with whom is the well of life. . . ." [17]

Whenever he argued against the Pelagian idea that men can and must obey God's law, therefore, Augustine argued for the absolute necessity of grace. One could wish that the debate had stopped there; but he had also to combat the Pelagian thesis that Adam's sin injured no one but himself and their allied theory that newborn infants are therefore in the same state of innocence as Adam before the Fall. These ideas clearly challenged the Church's traditional teaching that infants as well as adults need baptism for the remission of sin. From first to last in his long line of anti-Pelagian writings, Augustine defended the tradition. Infants are properly baptized, he writes, for "the remission of sins which they have contracted by their very birth, owing to the corruption of their origin." [18]

This language is offensive to the modern ear, and little understood. It will never be understood if one bogs down (as Augustine himself did in some of his polemic) in such relatively secondary questions as what happens to babies when they die. The key to the importance of baptism lies rather in the idea of the unity of mankind. Augustine's thinking is always radically social. "No one," he believes, "can exist of himself." [19]

For Augustine as for Paul, Christ is the new being, the New Man. The unity of the new mankind in Christ is the starting point in his argument for the idea that all men share in the sin of Adam. Since Christ is the only one in whom all are regenerated, by analogy Adam is the only one in whom all have sinned. He is the Old Man, for Augustine as for Paul. The course of Augustine's thought runs back from Christ to Adam, and not conversely as did Pelagian thinking. "If it is imitation only that makes men sinners through Adam," he asks, "why does not imitation likewise alone make men righteous through Christ?" [20] Although in the fifth century Augustine certainly thought of Adam as a historical personage, "original sin" was essentially social sin, just as new life in Christ was essentially social life.

Baptism is the indispensable occasion of the gift of life in Augustine's thinking. It is at baptism that believers are incorporated into Christ and hence re-created, restored to authentic human being. When infants are baptized, Christ by his grace engrafts them also into his body, into "the whole Christ." Infants are not yet ready to imitate anyone; they are not yet able to believe or disbelieve. But they are counted among the faithful, Augustine says, not because of what they have done by themselves but "through those who answer for them when they are said to renounce the Devil and to believe in God." [21] It is not only the sponsors in baptism who affect the child in this manner but "the whole society of saints and believers," in whom the Holy Spirit dwells. The corporate will of "those whom the glowing flame of love has fused together" is effective for the child by virtue of their common participation in the Body of Christ.

Society and its members are not ever separate in Augustine's mind, and he looks at individual life and social life alike in the light of one moral law, the law of love. He can happily equate the stages of an individual's life with the stages of human history, as he does in the *Enchiridion,* and say that one law applies equally to both. All God's commandments are "embraced in love" and "rightly carried out only when the motive principle of action is the love of God and the love of our neighbor in God." [22]

The Pelagian controversy brought forth some of Augustine's longest discussions of human sin, and some of his deepest explorations of divine grace, but it did not always bring forth the best in Augustine. Augustine at his best writes of love. No one can speak adequately of his concern for society without turning to what is perhaps his greatest work, *The City of God.* Here, of course, the corporate nature of his thinking is most evident; and here he conceives of human society and of human destiny entirely in terms of love. A republic or a kingdom or a people is defined as "an assemblage of reasonable beings bound together by a common agreement as to the objects of love." [23] In order to discover the character of any people, Augustine says, one has only to observe what they love. With this single criterion, he accounts simultaneously for all human suffering and for what he believed is the only true human happiness:

Accordingly, two cities have been formed by two loves: the earthly by the love of self, even to the contempt of God; the heavenly by the love of God, even to the contempt of self. The former, in a word, glories in itself, the latter in the Lord. For the one seeks glory from men; but the greatest glory of the other is God. . . . And therefore the wise men of the one city, living according to man, have sought for profit to their own bodies or souls, or both. . . . But in the other city there is no human wisdom, but only godliness, which offers due worship to the true God, and looks for its reward in the society of the saints. . . .[24]

Evil is both common and serious to the Bishop of Hippo, but it does not have the last word.

CHAPTER 9

Reason and Revelation

"I solemnly swear to tell the truth, the whole truth, and nothing but the truth, so help me God." Have you ever stopped to analyze this familiar oath? On critical inspection the words appear so pretentious as to be absurd. In order that the jury may establish what truly happened, the witness promises to tell the whole truth. Where was he last August 1? On a universal scale, he has no idea. He has been whirling through space for a month since then. Would the jury care to be reminded of this fact?

And is it a fact? In the courtroom setting, hearsay evidence is out of order. The witness's senses tell him that the earth beneath him is flat and motionless; but sensory data are notoriously deceptive. In spite of the conflict with his everyday experience, he has accepted the evidence of scientists who tell him that the earth is constantly moving. So he knows that he does not know the whole answer.

The oath charges him, furthermore, to call on God to help him tell the truth. But does he know enough about deity to know whether it is of such a nature that it could offer help in truth-telling? Is it capable of this sort of personalized interest in what a man says? How does he know? If he took the words he recited literally, a scrupulous witness might well find himself tongue-tied.

Very few men today would ever volunteer to speak the whole truth. We are more modest in our claims to knowledge. Yet many men still value the idea of truth and try to know and tell it. If they reflect about it, they are confronted by serious questions. How does a man know anything? Does he live in a rational universe, where it makes sense to speak of knowing the truth at all? Is it a whole, or are there just relative truths, so that a man should speak only of scientific truth, or of psychological truth, or of religious truth? Should theologians perhaps dismiss any truth claim whatsoever, on the grounds that truth is a religiously irrelevant concept?

Such questions are independent of any formal concern for epistemology. They arise from the complexity of the scientific age in which we live. The spirit of that age makes it impossible for many people to accept the idea that there is any intelligible, unitary meaning in the cosmos. Ever since Galileo burst the bonds of a tidy, self-contained universe, men have found it increasingly difficult to entertain the notion that we live in a world governed by reason. Ever since Freud unveiled the subconscious, the doubts have grown stronger. The truly modern man, it has been said, is one who believes in the ultimate irrationality of everything.[1] Philosophers as different as Bertrand Russell and Jean Paul Sartre share the conviction that the universe is completely indifferent to man and his values, including the value of truth. By definition, the Christian has rejected this belief; therefore he is faced with two other problems—the problem of relating science to religion, and the concomitant problem of authority.

OUR APPROACHES TO KNOWLEDGE

Because the question of science and religion is usually posed in a false form, men of faith today (professional scientists as well as professional theologians) tend to deny vehemently the existence of a conflict between them. Too vehemently. Unless one is a biblical literalist, it is easy to demonstrate that there is no necessary abyss between established facts of geology, say, and the creation story of Genesis 1, or between theories of evolution and the story of Adam. But beyond this elementary level, a genuine conflict remains for most Christians. They are committed, on the one hand, to the concept that revelation provides trustworthy knowledge about ultimate reality. They are taught such respect for the scientific method, on the other hand, that it easily assumes exclusive rights to the province of human reason. Since neither God nor Santa Claus is subject to empirical verification, modern man almost inevitably puts them in the same class. Religion, he concludes, is the province of faith (usually qualified as blind), whereas knowledge is the product of scientific inquiry.

If one takes a second look at this conclusion, he must quickly acknowledge that it oversimplifies. In all areas of human knowing there is an element of faith. The presuppositions of both science and religion are beyond proof in the sense of laboratory demonstration. And in both science and religion one must trust reports of others. Much of what we call scientific knowledge is at odds with our own experience. We have time and talent to verify only a very small part of it by our own experimental investigation. For the most part, we merely trust the testimony of the experts. A revealed religion such as Christianity also offers alleged knowledge of reality, some of which is subject to experiential verification and some of which is not. But it is not self-evident how the two types of knowledge fit together. Is all truth of a piece?

Deep-seated individualism leads many Americans to distrust authoritarianism, and to confuse it with authority. Rejecting the former, they fail to see the necessity for the latter. One spokesman in the contemporary dialogue with Roman Catholicism calls the question of authority the Achilles heel of Protestantism.[2] Religious certainty, like any other certainty, poses a problem of authority. What sources of knowledge are genuinely trustworthy? How should a thinking Christian combine the evidence of his personal experience with the experience of others? What weight is he to give to human reason? What weight is he to give to the Bible? What place to a teaching Church?

Contemporary Christianity thinks about reason and revelation in four different ways. Although the terms in which the problem was posed were slightly different, the relationship between reason and revelation was also one of the central intellectual concerns of the twelfth and thirteenth centuries; and theologians then took the same four approaches. In thinking about man's knowledge of the truth, some Christian believers in both ages have settled for suppressing one source of knowledge. This answer has two forms. One gives major authority to revelation and lets reason say what it will, unheeded. The other gives major authority to reason and puts revelation in the back seat, to support rational conclusions as and when it can. The third and fourth ways both attempt to synthesize reason and revelation; but the third calls for a division of labor between them, assigning different but complementary functions to each. The fourth gives primacy to faith in all knowing, but considers reason a necessary partner with revelation in a joint search for knowledge.

REASON VS. REVELATION

The authority of the Church was undoubtedly a presupposition of the age we call medieval, but its theologians were intensely aware that Church authority could be questioned. Within that united Christendom which we are so prone to romanticize, three developments contributed to making them acutely conscious, in the twelfth and thirteenth centuries, of problems of reason and revelation. The first was renewed contact with another revealed religion. Although the Moslem advance into Europe had been decisively halted in the eighth century, Spain remained largely under Islamic control for the next three hundred years. With the capture of Toledo at the end of the eleventh century, the first great step was made in the Christian reconquest of Spain. By the end of the thirteenth century, Moslem territory had shrunk to the little coastal emirate of Granada. In the same period, the Crusades brought fresh encounters with Islam in the East, and fresh need to assert the truth of the Christian revelation as over against the revelation vouchsafed to the prophet Mohammed and embodied in the Qur'an.

Meanwhile the rise of the schools, and then of the universities, in Europe produced a growing body of human knowledge, and with it a growing desire to relate theology to other intellectual disciplines. The schoolmen exerted a conscious effort to make theology scientific. They sought to apply the principles of logic to the truths of revelation, to sharpen rational analysis of what the Church proposed for a man's belief.

And in the twelfth century, Christian Europe rediscovered Aristotle. Although his logic had been known all along, through the works of Boethius, the rest of Aristotelian thought first came to Latin Christians by way of the Islamic scholars in the Spanish universities. For such scholars, Aristotle created a sharp conflict between reason and revelation. What was one to do when Aristotle's conclusions seemed to contradict the Qur'an? In his treatise on *The Agreement of Religion and Philosophy,* the great Moslem philosopher Averroes explored the problem and decided that, for the philosopher only, the necessary demonstrations of reason are compelling, but that the philosopher is under no obligation to disturb the faith of common people for whom the materials of revelation provide sufficient certainty.[3]

When the Christian intellectuals made Aristotle "The Philosopher," they encountered the same problem, and some of them came to the same conclusion. Aristotle taught them, for example, that the world was eternal. Revelation taught them that it was created out of nothing "in the beginning." Some theologians at the University of Paris, confronted with two seeming irreconcilables, decided that they need not be harmonized. There can be such a thing as necessary conclusions from philosophy, they thought, which do not gibe with "the truth of God." The theories of these Latin Averroists, which led eventually to church condemnation of the study of Aristotle, provide an extreme example of a divorce between revelation and reason.

More representative of the age, and of the parallel positions in the modern world, are two major antagonists in the twelfth-century Church, Bernard of Clairvaux and Peter Abelard. In the conflict between them, Bernard is the great advocate of revelation, against Abelard, disciple of reason. Neither man wanted a complete divorce between reason and revelation, but each resolved tension in the marriage by giving one partner chief authority.

Christian believers who accept revelation unquestioningly have the simplest answer to the problem we are considering. As Etienne Gilson expresses it, they merely say, "since God has spoken to us, it is no longer necessary for us to think." [4] Bernard (1091-1153) shares some of this spirit, but it would be a mistake to dismiss him simply as a credulous anti-intellectual. He was not opposed to thought, but he was more concerned with action and with contemplation. As an activist, Bernard is said to have carried the twelfth century on his shoulders. When one weighs his reform of monastic life, his preaching of the Second Crusade, his diplomatic work to heal the papal schism, his fight against the new form of Manicheanism in southern France, along with his efforts to silence Peter Abelard, the description seems an apt one. As a contemplative and a mystic, Bernard was a man overwhelmed by the humility of love. He was utterly convinced that the way that leads to truth is Christ, and that the way that leads to Christ is humility.[5] To Bernard, meditation on the name of Jesus Christ was worth more than a thousand theological disputations.

Small wonder then that Bernard, who believed in mounting to truth by the way of humility, was shocked and disturbed by the arrogance of Peter Abelard. Abelard, the brilliant lecturer in theology at the University of Paris, had "the intelligence that would reach down a handful of stars from heaven and set them by his book to read by." [6] To Bernard he was "a man who does not know his own limitations, making void the virtue of the cross by the cleverness of his words." [7] The Abbot of Clairvaux was always opposed to leaning too much on human reasoning.

Bernard was so disturbed by the critical spirit which Abelard was engendering in the Church that he agreed to personal debate with him before a council of bishops at Sens in 1140. Before and after that council, he wrote numerous letters denouncing the errors of his opponent. He has fault to find with certain specific doctrines, but it is Abelard's general approach to theology that is the real root of the problem as Bernard sees it. Writing to his friend Cardinal Haimeric, the Abbot complains that Abelard "tries to explore with his reason what the devout mind grasps at once with a vigorous faith. Faith believes, it does not dispute. But this man, apparently holding God suspect, will not believe anything until he has first examined it with his reason." [8]

Reporting to Pope Innocent after Sens, he charges that Abelard "insults the Doctors of the Church by holding up the philosophers for exaggerated praises. He prefers their ideas and his own novelties to the doctrines of faith and the Catholic Fathers." [9] Bernard clearly believes that the faith was once for all delivered to the saints and has been cherished by the Church ever since. This should be enough to satisfy even Abelard. But instead,

. . . mere human ingenuity is taking on itself to solve everything, and leave nothing to faith. It is trying for things above itself, prying into things too strong for it, rushing into divine things, and profaning rather than revealing what is holy. Things closed and sealed, it is not opening but tearing asunder, and what it is not able to force open, that it considers to be of no account and not worthy of belief.[10]

Peter Abelard (1079-1142) was definitely not satisfied with the received faith. His approach to revelation is summed up in the title of one of his best-known works—*Sic et Non.* He knew full well that the Bible and the fathers answer yes and no to the questions men ask of them; he collected their conflicting testimony to demonstrate the problem. "Here begin sentences taken from the Holy Scriptures which seem opposed to each other . . . ," *Sic et Non* starts out.[11] There follow over 150 theological questions answered both ways. Yet Abelard was not rejecting the idea of revelation. He did not substitute the dogma of God's total silence, as a modern rationalist might, leaving men's minds with only a rumor about ultimate being. He was not recanting under pressure from authority when he wrote, "I do not want to be a philosopher at the price of being rejected by Paul; nor yet an Aristotle at the price of being rejected by Christ, for there is no other name under heaven whereby I can be saved." [12]

What was he trying to do then? No one could answer the question better than Helen Waddell has done in her unforgettable novel *Peter Abelard*. She re-creates the moment when the idea for *Sic et Non* is born, as Abelard remembers the teachers he has studied under and triumphed over:

Sheep every one of them, with their meek faces, browsing over and over the old close-bitten pastures, with their "St. Augustine saith. . . . St. Jerome saith. . . . The Blessed Gregory saith. . . ." As if one could not prove anything, and deny it, and prove it back again, out of St. Augustine alone. Sometime he would do it, for a testimony unto them. Pit the Fathers one against the other. Smash the whole blind system of authority and substitute . . . Master Peter Abelard? said the mocking voice within him. He shook his head, suddenly humble. Not that. Not that. But a reasonable soul. *The spirit of man is the candle of the Lord.* Abelard shuddered and was still. It was about him again, the dark immensity, the pressure of some greatness from without upon his brain, and that within which struggled to break through to it. *I said, Ye are gods.*[13]

Where the evidence of scripture and tradition conflicted, Abelard believed that man was to use his God-given reason in judgment. For it was because of reason, as Abelard understood it, that man was said to be made in the image of God.

Bernard's distrust of reason and his confidence in revelation put him close to naïve believers of today who seem to equate revelation with a long-distance telephone call from God. Abelard's honest facing of the conflicts in scripture and tradition is a necessary corrective to this fideism, and a treasured witness to the art of Christian doubt. But his great trust in the capacity of men's minds is difficult to share in an age which knows as much as ours about individual rationalization and communal brain-washing. The remaining two ideas

which Christians have held and still hold about the relation
between reason and revelation take the limitations of both
more fully into account. The medieval spokesman for the
first is Thomas Aquinas; for the second, Anselm of Canterbury.

ASSENT THROUGH SCIENCE AND FAITH

No man's thought ever fits as neatly into a pigeonhole as
his interpreters would like. Even Thomas Aquinas (1225-
1274), one of the most consistent and systematic thinkers
known to Christian history, defies efforts to label him once
and for all. His eucharistic hymns, for example, call into
question all unqualified statements that he achieves a completely balanced synthesis of reason and revelation. Nevertheless, in his systematic works he speaks with clarity and
finality for a division of labor between them. Science and
faith, Thomas believed, are two specifically different kinds
of assent.[14]

Defenders of this position in the modern world want to
distinguish spheres of religion and science by clear definition
of their respective roles. In a letter printed in a popular magazine not long ago, a Jewish scientist argued that science does
not require our belief in any statements except those that
report direct sense perceptions, and that it cannot command
our disbelief on matters outside its stated field.[15] Surprised
as the writer might be with the designation, this is the voice
of a Thomist in the twentieth century. For to Thomas
Aquinas, faith is assent of the intellect to that which the
intellect does not see to be true. *Scientia,* knowledge, is assent
to what the intellect does see to be true, ultimately on the
basis of sensory perception.

Gilson pictures a Thomist as "a man who does not like
to believe what he can know, and who never pretends to
know what can be but believed." [16] In support of a separa-

tion between the stated fields of science and religion, our
modern Thomist went on to say that religion, of course, need
not be irrelevant to the scientist. The original Thomist
agreed. His word portrait is finished, therefore, with the qual-
ification "and yet a man whose faith and knowledge grow
into an organic unity because they both spring from the same
divine source." [17]

Today or in the day of the master, Thomists rest on the
principle of non-contradiction. Knowledge which comes from
science, and beliefs from revelation, are parts of one whole
truth of God. Both are necessary. In his *Summa,* directed
especially to the Moslem intellectuals—translated today under the title *On the Truth of the Catholic Faith*[18]—Thomas
spells out with precision the distinction between natural
reason and revelation. He is writing theology; and although
theology is a science whose conclusions necessarily follow
from its principles, those principles are articles of faith. So,
for that matter, are the first principles of all sciences, in
Thomas' opinion. Nevertheless, some true knowledge about
God is available to natural reason.

He divides his work into two distinct parts—the first
dealing with truths which faith proposes and reason investi-
gates, the second dealing with truths of faith above reason,
for which reason can bring forth probable but not demon-
strable arguments. Reason, in St. Thomas' mind, can tell a
man that God is, and a great deal about what God does. It
can also tell him about the man God creates, and about that
man's meaning and purpose. But it can never enable a man
to reach his proper end, to fulfill his true purpose. For that,
the vision of God, revelation, is absolutely necessary. Only
through revelation can a man come to believe the saving
truth of a triune God incarnate in Jesus Christ, whose means
of grace are given through the sacraments of his Church. Such
truth, however, is not opposed to reason, even though reason
can never demonstrate it conclusively.

In Thomas' system, reason and revelation form a perfectly matched couple. They complement each other every step of the way. Even as reason supports revelation in her sphere, by bringing forth probable arguments in favor of facts which are originally beyond his grasp, so revelation assists reason in his province. Under the right conditions, human reason *can* discover many things about God, but only a few intellectuals have the capacity and the time to use it for this purpose. And even their conclusions could be mixed with error.[19] The Word of God, to which faith assents, makes up for these deficiencies of natural reason. So, for Thomas, there is complete harmony between reason and revelation, but in the end revelation does most of the work.

FAITH LEADING TO REASON

Our fourth and final representative almost tips the balance of responsibility in the opposite direction. Anselm (1033-1109), who reluctantly became Archbishop of Canterbury in 1093, was the first great theologian of the Middle Ages. His starting place was faith. With Augustine, he was convinced that unless you believe you will not be able to understand. Therefore the watchword of Anselm's position is *Credo ut intelligam*. I believe *in order that. . . .* Anselm's faith is always a faith seeking understanding.

It was in search of understanding that Anselm launched into the intellectual exercise for which he is most widely known, his celebrated ontological proof for the existence of God. It is found in his *Proslogion,* which bears the subtitle *Fides Quaerens Intellectum.* Just what Anselm achieved with his logical argument (that, as "that than which nothing greater can be conceived," God must necessarily exist) is a matter of debate. Some interpreters insist that he was not trying to prove anything; he was simply meditating on divine being, trying to show what is implicit in that very notion.

Despite various efforts recently to rehabilitate Anselm's argument, the sympathies of most lay theologians remain with Anselm's first critic, Gaunilon the Fool. Gaunilon retorted that he could conceive of a perfect island in the Atlantic, but that the reality of such an island did not follow merely from his having an idea of it.

For our purposes, the important thing is not the validity of the argument, but the fact of it. Anselm knew that philosophical dialectic was not the source of faith, but he believed it was a useful and even beautiful instrument in the service of faith. Reason (which is essentially logic for Anselm) functions in the context of faith; but it must function. To seek understanding is part of the nature of faith. Just because we possess the certainty of faith, we must hunger after a reason for the faith that is in us.

Anselm's attitude toward revelation and reason has had a decisive influence on one of the most profound and prolific living theologians, Karl Barth. In the preface to his study of Anselm, Barth declares that it is "a vital key, if not the key" to an understanding of the whole process of thought in his monumental *Church Dogmatics*.[20] Barth explains that we approach Anselm's position when we say that, by its very nature, faith desires knowledge. *"Credo ut intelligam* means: It is my very faith itself that summons me to knowledge."[21] For Anselm, the God in whom we have faith is Truth itself, and the author of all that we call truth apart from him. From his way of relating reason and revelation, it follows that the faithful use reason fully, in order that they may have joy in their believing.

In all ages some Christians have joined Bernard of Clairvaux in believing the authority of the Bible and the Church, no matter how absurd revealed truth might seem to the human intellect. In all ages some Christians have joined Peter Abelard in doubt of this authority. Since God has given men minds, they believe, they should use them in rigorous critique of any proposition that seems unreasonable. With Anselm and Aquinas, other Christians cannot be content with any sort of intellectual schizophrenia. They are drawn to seek wholeness. Many today are convinced, with Thomas, that there can be no final contradiction between the knowledge acquired by man's natural reason and the supranatural truth revealed by God. Less confident than Anselm that all the truths of revelation can be demonstrated by logic, many others today start in faith nevertheless, on a lifelong search for understanding.

CHAPTER 10

Faith and Works

What shall I do to be saved? The question sounds archaic in our ears. Market research shows no great demand for a product labeled salvation. We are looking, to be sure, for health. One doesn't have to inventory the medicine cabinet in the fabulous Glass family bathroom to be convinced of that. A stop in front of the drug counter in any store will do the trick. We are also looking for escape from nervous tension. One doesn't have to marshal statistics on ulcers and alcoholism, much less on mental hospitals and psychiatric clinics, to demonstrate pervasive dis-ease. Just a quick survey of the mental health titles on any paperback or magazine rack offers enough evidence. We welcome new slogans, because the diagnostic phrases so quickly lose their fizz, but we know that whatever we call it, ours is an Age of Anxiety.

One approach to life in such an age is the frenetic. A current radio commercial captures this response in its insidious jingle "Busy, busy, busy; run, run, run." All the latest

electrical equipment may help a woman "get things done";
but it does not usually give her time to put her feet up and
wonder whether they really need doing, because one more
committee meeting and one more party are too valuable as
ways of covering up inner disquietude. A popular alternative
to overcrowding the calendar is the tranquilizer, although not
necessarily the kind that comes in bottles. There are dozens
of recommended routes to serenity, all of them telling the
patient just what he should do to get there.

Even the most superficial critic of our culture realizes
that members of the Christian Church today are no marked
exception to the common social malaise. The vast quantity
of soul-searching self-criticism among those who profess and
call themselves Christians is, rather, one of its symptoms. We
acknowledge that the schedule of weekly events in the average
parish bulletin is ridiculous, but we prefer to be busy. We
sneer at certain brands of peace-of-mind religion, partly because we enjoy writhing in our own spiritual discomfort; but
at the same time we accept a reasonable facsimile if it helps
us deal with the guilt feelings which come from being no less
anxious than anyone else. Christians or non-Christians, we
cannot accept ourselves. We are all afraid that no one else will
accept us either.

Americans in the second half of the twentieth century
are certainly not the first men to worry because they are living in a sick civilization. Historians find comparable concern
in whatever period they happen to specialize in. No period in
the history of Christian thought, however, bears any closer
kinship to the troubled spirit of our time than that profoundly restless age of Reformation. Churchmen in the six-
teenth century were caught in an anxious struggle for peace
of conscience. They believed that God demanded that they *do*
something to get in a right relationship with him. The
Church's emphasis on penance and purgatory was a result of
this root religious problem, not a cause. For thinking Chris-

tians, the problem was intensified by the philosophical developments of the recent past. The new mood of nominalism made it difficult to trust meekly in a benevolent God, for now it was easier to think of him in terms of arbitrary will. He might decide at any moment, so to speak, for you or against you. How could a man be sure that he was accepted?

JUSTIFICATION BY FAITH ALONE

For their culturally conditioned form of human anxiety, the Reformers found an answer. In its capsule form, the answer is called justification by faith. In its general understanding of God's response to human need, the answer undergirds all sixteenth-century Protestant thought, in England as well as on the Continent.

Martin Luther (1483-1546) did not invent the idea of justification by faith; but he was chiefly responsible for bringing it to the center of Christian attention. His own personal problems undoubtedly helped him to do so. Because many shallow interpretations of the great reformer's thought have come from would-be psychologists, who analyze his personality, this is an unfashionable statement. One cannot explain any man's ideas adequately just by way of his biography. But by ignoring the man, one can also miss the ideas.

The young professor of theology who posted some discussion topics on his university bulletin board in 1517 was an Augustinian monk, who had entered the monastery twelve years earlier, when he was twenty-two. Even then he was burdened by a great sense of sin, and by periodic attacks of dread, both of death and of judgment. Although this aspect of his monastic career is sometimes exaggerated, Luther's superior in the Order is said to have found him overscrupulous in his frequent use of confession and in his extraordinary acts of penance. Luther himself suggests reasons for such self-

discipline. He was trying to become sinless, for that was what
he thought the Christianity of his day demanded:

They constrained men to work well so long, until they should
feel in themselves no sin at all. Whereby they gave occasion to
many (which, striving with all their endeavour to be perfectly
righteous, could not attain thereunto) to become stark mad. . . .
Which thing had happened unto me also, if Christ had not mercifully looked upon me, and delivered me out of this error.[1]

"Our human weakness, conscious of its sins, finds nothing
more difficult to believe," he wrote in 1520, "than that it is
saved or will be saved." [2] Gnawing self-doubt found the answer, "Faith alone sets the conscience at peace." [3]

Luther came to his great and liberating insight by studying the Bible. His Order sent him to teach at the University
of Wittenberg in 1512. Some Luther scholars believe that he
had made his essential discovery as early as the end of his
first year as a teacher, after lecturing on the psalms. He had
certainly made it by 1518, when he lectured on Paul's letter
to the Romans; and it is Paul who provides the key to Luther's
understanding of the Christian faith. The Epistle to the Romans, Luther believed, "is in truth the most important document in the New Testament, the gospel in its purest expression. Not only is it well worth a Christian's while to know it
word for word by heart, but also to meditate on it day by day.
It is the soul's daily bread, and can never be read too often,
or studied too much." [4]

It is next to impossible for any post-Reformation Christian to read Romans without using Luther's spectacles and
hence concentrating primarily on Paul's doctrine of justification developed in that letter. Justification is a metaphor bor-
rowed from the courts, and denotes the status "not guilty,"
declared in the right. Paul writes, "For we hold that a man
is justified by faith apart from works of law" (*Rom. 3:28*). It

is Luther who adds, in his German translation, the emphatic *allein*; a man is justified "by faith alone." But the difference is slight. Both men are thinking about the fact that what a man has done cannot acquit him.

Whether the man is Paul, blameless (he says) if judged by the requirements of Pharisaic Judaism, or Luther, obedient to the minutiae of the monastic rule by which he lived, he still falls short. Paul specified that all men fall short of the glory of God. Judged by the standard of perfect righteousness, all men are guilty, always. If one cannot ever do enough to satisfy himself, how can he hope to satisfy a judge who expects perfection?

Luther's answer, discovered in Paul, is simple. He can't. But he doesn't have to. The principle is all wrong. God does not judge a man on this basis, and so a man does not have to judge himself on this basis either. On what principle, then, can a man be accepted? The shorthand tags of Reformation theology are misleading at this point; Luther's answer to this second question is more complicated than "by faith alone." In his treatise on "The Freedom of a Christian Man," he puts it this way:

For the person is justified and saved, not by works or laws, but by the Word of God, that is, by the promise of his grace, and by faith, that the glory may remain God's, who saved us not by works of righteousness which we had done, but by virtue of his mercy by the word of his grace when we believed.[5]

Three parts of this answer are absolutely essential in Luther's understanding of justification: the Word of God, by grace, through faith.

The Word of God, for Martin Luther as for Christian theology generally, is Jesus Christ. The Word is known through the Bible, but it can never be equated with the Bible. "The Word," Luther wrote in the same exposition of Christian liberty, "is the gospel of God concerning his Son, who was made flesh, suffered, rose from the dead. . . ." [6] No person can earn God's approval by his own efforts, but Jesus Christ has already earned it for him. If a single-phrase summary of Luther's key idea were ever necessary, it would be more accurate to say, not justification by faith, but justification by Jesus Christ. "For our sakes, He has become God's 'mercy seat,' and so God forgives all the sins we have committed in the past." [7]

Grace, in Luther's thought, is primarily this forgiveness. The word forgiveness could easily be substituted for grace both times in the definition of justification quoted above. Its essential character, however, is that of a true gift, totally undeserved and totally unearned. God is not handing out merit badges, but—almost literally—Christmas presents.

Faith enters the Lutheran account of a man's acquittal only in the third and last place, and it was even then a term which required different connotations from those ordinarily attached to it. In much sixteenth-century usage, faith meant intellectual assent to a proposition. Not so in Luther's mind. He made a sharp distinction between the Latin words *assensus* (belief) and *fiducia,* which means trust, reliance, or assurance. He describes faith as "a lively and unshakeable confidence, a belief in the grace of God so assured that a man would die a thousand deaths for its sake. This kind of confidence in God's grace, this sort of knowledge of it, makes us joyful, high-spirited, and eager in our relations with God and with all mankind. That is what the Holy Spirit effects through faith." [8]

When Martin Luther discovered what for him was a new idea of Christian faith, therefore, a great sense of freedom took the place of anxious striving to make himself acceptable. He was, he realized, already accepted. Jesus Christ had done all that needed doing. All that was left for him to do was to accept the gift of forgiveness in complete confidence. Indeed, the confidence, the faith, was itself a part of the gift. In Luther's understanding, man is completely passive in everything which has to do with his being in the right relationship with God. He does not have to rush around looking for faith as a substitute activity, a new form of anxious striving. Luther insists that men are brought to faith and strengthened in faith by the work of God himself, through the preaching of the Word and through the holy sacraments.

GOOD WORKS THROUGH SANCTIFICATION

In discovering justification by faith, Martin Luther believed that he had rediscovered the true Christian gospel. His fellow theologians in sixteenth-century Protestantism agreed with him, among them Thomas Cranmer, Archbishop of Canterbury under Henry VIII of England. Although Henry denounced the pernicious doctrine of Luther and thus won from the Pope the title "Defender of the Faith," Cranmer had tremendous respect for the German reformer. In fact, he increasingly felt a kinship with all the Continental theologians, some of whom he had come to know when they were visiting lecturers in the English universities. While the Council of Trent was in session, and after it had anathematized certain of the extreme Protestant statements about justification, Cranmer tried to assemble a rival council of European Protestant leaders, to compare ideas and to arrive at a common statement of their own doctrine in response. In 1549, and again in 1552, he wrote to persuade Luther's successor, Melanchthon, to attend such a conference of those "in whose churches the doctrine of the gospel has been restored and purified." [9]

What Cranmer called the purified gospel was one which emphasized a Lutheran idea of faith in relation to works. *The Homily on Salvation,* officially approved for public reading in English parish churches at the time (and thought to

be by Cranmer), explains that three things must concur in
our justification: God's grace, Christ's offering, and our true
and lively faith in the merits of Christ, which yet is not ours
but God's working in us. Simply believing *that* the articles
of faith about Christ are true is not enough; even devils believe them and still remain devils. True Christian faith is
defined as "a sure trust and confidence in God's merciful
promises." [10]

Cranmer's respect for the Lutheran understanding of this
central doctrine led him to incorporate in his forty-two suggested articles of faith for the Church of England a statement
about justification in very nearly the same words as those
used in Lutheran confessions of faith. The definition remained in the Thirty-Nine Articles adopted in Queen Eliza-
beth's reign:

We are accounted righteous before God, only for the merit of our
Lord and Saviour Jesus Christ by Faith, and not for our own
works or deservings. Wherefore, that we are justified by Faith
only, is a most wholesome Doctrine, and very full of comfort. . . .[11]

Strong emphasis on man's passivity can easily lead to an
irresponsible kind of quietism. If good works have no value
in changing a man's status in the eyes of God, the question
inevitably arises, why bother? Luther, as had Paul before
him, fully realized the danger of this misunderstanding and
did his best to counteract it. Man's good deeds can never
merit his salvation, but they are nevertheless essential to the
Christian life. In fact, they are natural fruits of faith. In the
preface to his commentary on Romans, Luther explains:

The man of faith, without being driven, willingly and gladly
seeks to do good to everyone, serve everyone, suffer all kinds of
hardships, for the sake of the love and glory of the God who has
shown him such grace. It is impossible, indeed, to separate works

from faith, just as it is impossible to separate heat and light from fire.[12]

This is a new kind of doing, however, and "clean contrary to moral doing."

Cranmer echoes the same insistence on good works as the necessary consequence of a true and lively faith. Our works never justify us. Nevertheless "we do not mean that we should be idle and that nothing is required on our part afterward." Faith in Christ must bring forth a life according to God's commandments. Indeed, a man must "study to do good to every man."

In spite of such efforts to keep man aware of the importance of human actions, the Protestants were so horrified at the prevailing popular idea of earning salvation that they defined all works done apart from faith as having "the nature of sin." [13] It is not surprising that the Roman Catholic polemic of the day continually includes the charge that the Protestants undermine good works. The official pronouncements of Trent specifically repudiate the Protestant thesis that "all works before justification, for whatever reason they were done, are in truth sins and deserve the hatred of God." [14]

In view of this misunderstanding, and partly as a result of the polemic, the second and third generations of Reformation theologians gradually talk once more, along with justification, about the complementary doctrine traditionally called sanctification. In England this accompanies a conscious effort not only to retain continuity with the primitive Church but also to affirm the whole Christian faith. As John Jewel expressed it in 1564, "For if we deny any part of the gospel of Jesus Christ before men, he on the other side will deny us before his Father." [15] Writing for Roman Catholics, Jewel tries directly to counteract their criticisms of the Protestant stand on good works. He therefore quotes the homily statement that true faith cannot be idle and adds, "Thus therefore teach we the people . . . that the Spirit of sanctification is in our bodies and that Christ himself doth dwell in our hearts." [16]

AN ATTEMPT TO REBALANCE FAITH AND WORKS

Some twenty years later Richard Hooker (1554-1600), a young theologian whom Jewel had sponsored at Oxford, delivered a lecture on the subject of faith and works in his first year as Master of the Temple, where he was speaking to England's budding lawyers. Men were still sharpening their wits on theological debate, in what was virtually a spectator sport; it was an era which even established chairs of "controversial theology" in its universities. But instead of debating primarily against Roman Catholics, Hooker is now preaching in a time of controversy with the Puritans. His clerical colleague at the Temple, Walter Travers, was an avowed Calvinist and sharply critical of Hooker's theology. Isaac Walton records their conflict in his "Life of Mr. Richard Hooker": "for as one hath so pleasantly exprest it, 'the forenoon sermon spake Canterbury, and the afternoon, Geneva.' " [17]

When Canterbury spoke in the person of Richard Hooker, he delivered "A Learned Discourse on Justification, Works, and How the Foundation of Faith is Overthrown." The whole long lecture reflects that calm and balanced temper of mind which earned for Hooker the title "judicious." But three points are particularly noteworthy as showing the development on English soil of thought about justification by faith.

In the first place, Hooker admits flatly that much of the controversy between Protestant and Papist had become childish on both sides. "It is a childish cavil wherewith in the matter of justification our adversaries do greatly please themselves," he wrote, "exclaiming, that we tread all Christian virtues under our feet and require nothing in Christians but

faith; because we teach that faith alone justifieth." [18] But it
was equally childish for Protestants to think that when Roman Catholics talked of works they were overthrowing the
idea that salvation is through Jesus Christ. Travers denounced this sermon as too charitable toward the Roman
Church. Hooker's spirit in controversy is indicated in his
closing words: "Be it that Cephas hath one interpretation,
and Apollos hath another; that Paul is of this mind and Bar-
nabas of that; if this offend you, the fault is yours. Carry
peaceable minds. . . ." [19]

In the second place, Hooker's sermon on justification
regularly mentions sanctification in close juxtaposition to justification. He is trying to broaden the perspective, to avoid
too exclusive attention to one idea: "We ourselves do not
teach Christ alone, excluding our own faith unto justification; Christ alone, excluding our own works, unto sanctification; Christ alone excluding the one or the other as unneces-
sary unto salvation." [20] He distinguishes between two kinds
of righteousness: "That whereby we are justified is perfect,
but not yet inherent; that whereby we are sanctified, inherent
but not yet perfect." [21] After a long discussion of New Testament evidence on the subject of faith and works, he even tries
to reconcile Paul with James, whom Luther had wanted to
exclude from his canon of scripture for teaching that faith
without works is dead. They are talking about two different
things, Hooker argues, and God gives us both. He accepts us
as righteous in Christ, and he works Christian righteousness
in us.[22]

But in the third place, the judicious Richard Hooker,
irenic in spirit and eager to take an inclusive view, yet refuses
to allow for one instant the idea that God operates on the
Brownie point system, or that man can solve his problem by
any other do-it-yourself principle. Of works, he says plainly
and forcefully, "The best things we do have somewhat in
them to be pardoned. How then can we do any thing meri-

torious, and worthy to be rewarded . . . ? Wherefore, we acknowledge a dutiful necessity of doing well, but the meritorious dignity of doing well we utterly renounce." [23] Of faith, Hooker speaks with less clarity, often sounding as if he understood it, not in the strong Reformation sense of trust and confidence, but rather in the limited sense of intellectual assent to conceptual statements. It grieves Hooker that even men of such great capacity and judgment as Sir Thomas More could have misunderstood the Reformers' idea of justification by faith, thinking that now faith became just a new basis for reward. To More's mistaken interpretation of *sola fide*, Hooker replies, "God doth justify the believing man, yet not for the worthiness of his belief, but for his [Christ's] worthiness which is believed." [24]

The meaning Hooker gives to faith seems to have shrunk in contrast with that given it by Luther and Cranmer, even as the role of works seems to have grown. If Lutheranism always stands in danger of quietism, Anglicanism always stands in danger of Pelagian moralism. But to all these sixteenth-century theologians one thing was certain. Nothing we can do will deliver us from our own tense frenzy or from our own twilight existence: that salvation is by Christ alone. The foundation of faith which must not be overcome, according to Hooker's learned discourse on the subject, is the object of faith: for faith "neither justifieth, nor is; but ceaseth to be faith when it ceases to believe, that Jesus Christ is the only Saviour of the world." [25]

PART III
REASON AND RELEVANCE

CHAPTER 11

The Language of Faith

Peter once tried to explain Christian behavior to Jews assembled at Jerusalem for Pentecostal celebration; St. Paul, to commend Christian thinking to Athenians assembled at the Areopagus for philosophic discussion. Christians ever since have continued the effort to interpret their faith to both believers and non-believers. About A.D. 150 Justin, called the Martyr, addressed an *Apology* for Christian faith to the Emperor, the Senate, and the whole Roman people, using an already hallowed literary form of philosophic propaganda and appealing from the outset to what "sound reason" required. In 1564, John Jewel used the same form and the same appeal in his *Apology of the Church of England,* trying to persuade the heirs of Rome that those who had left Rome were "not all mad."

APOLOGETIC THEOLOGY

The work of the apologist is never ended. Each generation of Christians is called upon to express the gospel in the language of its own time and place. In each generation, the men who try to do so must appeal to men's intelligence. Justin and Jewel, and the apologists in the fourteen centuries between them, were confident that reason would support their case. Even Tertullian, who insisted that he believed the Christian gospel because it was absurd, produced a classic *Apology* —the one, in fact, which Jewel chose as his own model. When the faithful are addressing men who do not share their own convictions about revelation, they always try to reason with them.

Richard Hooker, whom we met in the last chapter as a mediator between the extremes of faith and works, was acutely conscious that human reason is fallible. Yet Hooker continued to trust the operation of logic as fully as any medieval schoolman. He tried to convince the Puritans to accept, on the strength of it, the Anglican idea of church order and government; and his words are a superb expression of the decisive role traditionally assigned to reason as the third source of authority in theology:

Be it that there are some reasons inducing you to think hardly of our laws. Are those reasons demonstrative, are they necessary, or but mere probabilities only? An argument necessary and demonstrative is such, as being proposed unto any man and understood, the mind cannot choose but inwardly assent. Any one such reason dischargeth, I grant, the conscience and setteth it at full liberty. For the public approbation given by the body of this whole church unto those things which are established, doth make it but probable that they are good. And therefore unto a necessary proof that they are not good, it must give place.[1]

In our day, confidence in reason in this sense has rightly been shaken. Although appeal to reason has not been discarded, the focus of contemporary argument for the faith has shifted. Men ask first, not whether the Christian gospel is reasonable, but whether it is relevant. It is seldom put this

crassly, but the primary question asked of anyone who believes that Jesus died and was raised again is, "So what? What
difference does it make, if any, to my life or the life of my
nation and the world?" The question is perfectly valid. Recognizing its cogency, because they address the same question
to themselves, Christians try to answer it with relevance.
Christianity and. . . . One can complete the popular title
with phrases from the whole gamut of human experience and
human learning: sex, war, family life; the natural sciences,
the social sciences, the arts. But what should the Christian
apologist put into the exposition?

We tend to associate an apologist with someone who admits being in the wrong. An apology is so often just a polite
offer of excuses. We might do better to use the old word
apologia, which originally meant a defense made in courts of
justice, where one is innocent until proven guilty. But even
this has too narrow a connotation. An apologist is speaking in
behalf of something. With Cardinal Newman, the Christian
apologist is making an *apologia pro vita sua.*

If the Church is to have effective apologists in the modern world, it must also have apologetic theologians. The two
roles are different. Strictly speaking, apologetic theology is
the study of ways and means of defending the Christian faith.
It is the theory which precedes and undergirds the practice.
In its broader sense, apologetic theology is concerned with
disciplined thinking about communicating the gospel to contemporary civilization. As Canon Richardson explains it:

Apologetics deals with the relationship of the Christian faith to
the wider sphere of man's "secular" knowledge—philosophy,
science, history, sociology, and so on—with a view to showing
that faith is not at variance with the truth that these enquiries
have uncovered. In every age it is necessary that this task should
be undertaken; in a period of rapid developments in scientific
knowledge and of vast social change it becomes a matter of considerable urgency.[2]

Since Canon Richardson wrote these words, the pace of change has accelerated and the urgency has increased. Anyone who wants to communicate the gospel today must think about apologetic theology as such, because he must necessarily decide between competing theories of how to do it. One can practice an art without any knowledge of the theory behind it, of course; but in most cases people can do things better if they know what they are trying to do. Granted that I may drive a car without knowing what is going on under the hood; when something breaks down, I must either fix it myself or find a mechanic who knows what is wrong. If one mechanic thinks it is the valves, and another says it is only the spark plugs, and still a third tells me that it is hopeless to try to fix it, that I must turn it in on a new model, I have to make a decision. Which expert do I listen to? And if I decide on the new car, which model do I buy? All Christians who are trying to communicate the gospel today agree that apologetic techniques need a thorough overhaul. But when one goes to the theorists, he finds that they do not agree—either about the seriousness of the trouble or about the best ways and means to deal with it.

In these final chapters we shall try to introduce some of the current theorists and the recent practitioners of the art of defending Christian truth. Not all the men would think of themselves primarily as apologists or apologetic theologians in the technical sense, but they are all trying either to communicate the Christian gospel to its cultured despisers or to think directly about better ways and means of doing so.

THE SEARCH FOR EFFECTIVE THEOLOGICAL LANGUAGE

Contemporary theology must decide, in the first place, what language to use. Christians are called, as the old language has it, to witness to Christ. This must mean sometimes to speak about him. Granted that one can speak in a language other than words, and that the wrong words are often worse than silence; nevertheless, sooner or later words as such are called for. This is not unexpected in the faith which makes so much of the Word, but this traditional title simply illustrates the problem before us. What does it mean to anyone today just to see the word *Word* printed with a capital letter?

The task of the Christian is to speak to the culture in which he lives, in a language understood by the people. But at the same time, the task of the Christian is to be faithful to his Christian heritage, to speak in such ways that there is a genuine continuity between the contemporary expression and the Christ of whom he would speak. The double task raises two particular problems of language which deserve to be noted before we look at two persistent dangers in trying to solve them, and finally at two contemporary approaches to a new answer.

The first problem arises from the need to speak to our own culture. To what culture should one try to be relevant? C. P. Snow has sounded the deep chasm between the world of science and the world of the humanities, but there are more than two cultures to be considered. There are other canyons and fissures and cracks across the map of the contemporary intellectual world. Not only is the artist unable to speak to the scientist, but the bio-physicist is unable to talk to the chemist, or the political scientist to the sociologist, or the man who specializes in the nineteenth-century English novel to the man whose field is seventeenth-century English poetry. So "the academic world" acknowledges a multiversity where once there was a university, and its own isolation from "the business world" or "the entertainment world," each with its own multiplicities and its own jargons. No one denies the right of the specialist to his own precise terminology. In this matter, the theologian claims the same privilege as the lawyer or the psychiatrist or the physicist. But when the specialist wishes to speak to the non-specialist, what language is he to use?

The second problem arises from the need to express the received faith. Consider, for example, such an important Christian concept as the fatherhood of God. The public meaning of father in our day is vastly different from the public meaning of father in the Near East in ancient times. How does the Christian convince his hearers that he is not talking about the daddyhood of God? Each man also has his own private image of fatherhood, colored by his own personal experience. How does one know if the man to whom one is speaking had an alcoholic father who divorced his wife and rejected his son?

Aware of such problems of changing language and changing culture, some Christians decide to be modern at all costs. Communication to contemporary culture takes precedence over what is to be communicated. This decision always results in some kind of reductionism, some sacrifice of the gospel to relevance. At the beginning of this century, Adolf von Harnack, the great German historian of dogma, attempted to modernize the gospel in lectures to students at the University of Berlin. It is reported that at 7 A.M. there was standing room only in the lecture hall. A few years ago colorful paperback reprints of the lectures appeared on the newsstands under the title *What is Christianity?* [3] Those who bought and read, attracted by the look of relevance, found described there a Christianity almost indistinguishable from any other world religion. The attempt to strip the husk from the essential kernel left little more than the fatherhood of God and the brotherhood of man, neither of which is peculiar to Christianity. In Harnack's own generation, other attempts of the same sort produced the Modernism which still stands officially condemned by the Roman Church. Harnack is probably made a whipping boy too often, but it is hard to overlook such a blatant example of what can happen when the range of vision is limited to relevance.

Another set of blinders narrows the vision in the other direction. Recoiling from the perils of modernizing, many theologians fall into archaism. If I cannot translate the gospel into contemporary idiom without risk of distorting its meaning, I had better not try. I'll continue to sound as if a bearded God were up there on a cloud, stretching forth a mighty finger to waken life in the recumbent Adam. Let him who will, misunderstand. Archaism occurs in a biblicist form, among those who stand armored in the text of scripture and consider it sufficient answer to any question raised. It also occurs in a liturgical form, among those who think that the language of prayer and worship says all that needs to be said on any subject of the faith. Both forms of archaism can occur in sophisticated dress as well as in blinking neon.

Although in his great theological work, precisely titled *Church Dogmatics* for this reason, Karl Barth carefully disclaims any effort to communicate to the world outside the Church, he has been charged with such archaism, and not altogether without justice. Acclaimed by many as the greatest living theologian, he is virtually unintelligible to any non-Christian who can struggle through part of a chapter; and what he says seems almost totally irrelevant to any Christian who is not a professional theologian. Barth's gigantic theology of the Word of God is emphatically not apologetic theology, but it is fair to raise his name at this point simply to underscore heavily the problem of specialization already raised. Perhaps he did not consider it light reading, but certainly any man with a university education in the thirteenth century could understand Thomas Aquinas' *Summa Theologica*. Only a minute fraction of university graduates today can read and understand the exciting *Summa* of the twentieth century.

Have we reached an impasse? Is it possible to sound

relevant, to make sense, only by giving up talk of Christ crucified and raised from the dead? Or alternatively, if one has faith in the one "who for us men and for our salvation came down from heaven and was made man," is he doomed to remain incommunicado, separated from his own age by an impassable language barrier? Many honest thinkers see these as the only live options. But some are making rigorous attempts to think beyond this stalemate. The two most significant efforts to deal creatively with this problem today move in opposite directions. We shall listen briefly to a representative of each—Rudolf Bultmann, father of the Christ-without-myth school, and Austin Farrer, advocate of the rebirth of images.

DEMYTHOLOGIZING THE SCRIPTURES

As a New Testament scholar, Rudolf Bultmann knows better than most men that the psychology, the philosophy of history, and the cosmology of its writers are radically different from ours today. The problems of biblical hermeneutics, of interpreting scripture, become almost insoluble when the whole thought-world has changed. Nearly a generation ago Bultmann concluded that the first century thought in mythological terms, and that the terms which are derived from their thought are obsolete. He proposed demythologizing the Christian faith.

The awkward Germanic word *demythologizing* has been widely misunderstood, chiefly because of a common misapprehension that myth means a Santa Claus story about something everyone knows to be untrue. Although he uses the word variously, Bultmann does not think of myth in this condescending way. Mythological thought grows out of human attempts to express ultimate truth in pictorial, story form. Needless to say, the New Testament writers used the picture language of their own culture to express their own thinking,

as any writers must. But, since their mythical language is unintelligible today, Bultmann thinks much of it—whatever
does not materially affect the essential Christian kerygma—
can be dismissed. Some New Testament mythology, however,
is not simply accidental; it should not be discarded, but reinterpreted.[4]

In the first category Bultmann places the first-century
concept of a three-story universe with heaven above, the earth
in the middle, and the place of the departed under the earth.
Along with this cosmology as stage setting, the attendant ideas
of Christ's descent into hell, his ascent into heaven, and his
coming again on the clouds for a dramatic final judgment, are
irrelevant and can be forgotten. So, too, may the demons and
angels which inhabited the three-story universe, and Satan
as well.

Such stripping away of the biblical scenery is not designed just to make things easier for modern man, Bultmann
insists. He does not intend simply to be a modernist of the
sort we have associated with Harnack. "The purpose of de-
mythologization is not to make religion more acceptable to
modern man by trimming the traditional biblical texts," he
wrote,

but to make clearer to modern man what the Christian faith is.
He must be confronted with the issue of decision, to be provoked
to decision by the fact that the stumbling block to faith, the
skandalon, is peculiarly disturbing to man in general, not only
to modern man (modern man being only one species of man).
Therefore my attempt to demythologize begins true enough, by
clearing away the false stumbling blocks created for modern man
by the fact that his world view is determined by science.[5]

The program begins with clearing away the non-essential
mythological underbrush, in order that man can be confronted with the true problem. But even this stumbling block

is expressed in mythological language in the Christian tradition. The ideas of redemption and of incarnation, for example, are also obsolescent ways of expressing the revelation of God. Such material myth, Bultmann proposes to restate in contemporary terms, because in their present form they are too open to false objectification as doctrines about past events. When revelation becomes doctrine in this sense, it loses its truth for him. "What I am fighting against," Bultmann declares,

is just this fixation of God as an objective entity, against misconceiving the revelation as an act accomplished once and for all. . . . What matters is that the incarnation should not be conceived of as a miracle that happened about 1950 years ago, but as an eschatological happening, which, beginning with Jesus, is always present in the words of men proclaiming it to be a human experience.[6]

How does one accomplish this? Bultmann chooses to use the terms of modern existentialism, and especially the categories of the philosopher Martin Heidegger. They are appropriate to the expression of the true Christian kerygma, he feels, because they are always personal, and appeal, as the Christian revelation must, to selfhood, to authenticity, to actual being. Rightly understood, God's revelation is not a communication of teachings, ethical or historical or philosophical, but it is

God speaking directly to me, assigning me each time to the place that is allotted me before God, i.e., summoning me in my humanity, which is null without God, and which is open to God only in the recognition of its nullity. Hence there can be only one "criterion" for the truth of revelation, namely, this, that the word which claims to be the revelation must place each man before a decision—the decision as to how he wants to understand himself; as one who wins his life and authenticity by his own resources, reason, and actions, or by the grace of God.[7]

Bultmann's reinterpretation of the Christian revelation puts a bracket around the cross. The kerygma of the death and resurrection of Christ is never treated as mythological in precisely the same way as other New Testament events. He insists that the Christian message is bound to a historical tradition and looks back to a historical figure but only as evidence of the word of God. Christ must not be regarded as merely a past phenomenon, but as the ever present word of God, calling men to decision.

A collection of the books and articles developing Bultmann's proposals or disagreeing with them would already exceed a five-foot shelf. In general, the criticisms fall into two classes, some concentrating on his demythologizing, and some on his existentialist reinterpretation. Some critics find that he uses the word *myth* so loosely and ambiguously that he does not ever deal adequately with mythological thinking. They believe efforts might better be directed to deeper understanding of the nature of such thought and of the language in which it is expressed.[8] Others, who have little quarrel with the need for demythologizing biblical faith, find that Bultmann's restatement does not do the job adequately. Most frequently heard have been the charges that his extreme emphasis on the personal decision of faith individualizes the Christian understanding of life, ignoring its communal nature; and that his focus on the death-resurrection event excludes the broad biblical interest in the whole created order. In other words, that he divorces man from society, and history from nature—leaving an impoverished Christianity.

THE REBIRTH OF BIBLICAL IMAGES

In direct antithesis to Bultmann, other theologians concerned with religious language today recommend (if one uses the word mythical in its broadest way) not de- but re-mythologizing. No disagreement exists between them over the fact that the Bible is written in a language which is no longer our language, and that therefore Christians must do something other than quote scripture if anyone is to know what they are talking about. But instead of a new language adopted from one particular form of contemporary philosophy, these men think that what is needed is a rebirth of the Christian images. The phrase comes from the Anglican theologian Austin Farrer, one of many contemporary Christians calling for a re-creation of the human imagination.

In his Bampton lectures at Oxford, published in 1948 under the title *The Glass of Vision,* Dr. Farrer explores the relationship among the languages of metaphysics, poetry, and Holy Scripture. His thesis is well foreshadowed in the quotation from I Corinthians which appears on his title page: "Now we see through a glass darkly." But the words from the familiar King James Version conjure up in many of us the image only of a dirty window. St. Paul's meaning, and Farrer's, come better through the New English Bible translation: "Now we see only puzzling reflections in a mirror." The difference is incidentally a superb illustration of the problem of changing language. Between 1611 and 1962, progress brings picture windows to the home, the looking glass is relegated to the fairy story, and we lose the key to Paul's metaphor.

What Farrer is arguing in the lectures is that human beings talking about the fundamental mysteries of life necessarily use the language of analogy, metaphor, symbol, figure, and image, because they have no other for the purpose. Scientists measure and classify the particularities of our environment with their respective disciplines' own yardsticks, dictated by what is to be measured. They can use precise descriptive terms. Philosophers ask questions of the utmost generality, such as "What is the nature of the knowing act?" or "What is the relation of the self to the body?" In such questions, one is really asking, "What is it like?" One tries to answer by describing it in relation to something else. Is knowing, for example, something like seeing? We try the analogy of the physical eye. In discussion of the mysteries of existence, Farrer believes, "we are condemned to sheer irreducible analogy, the attempt, never really possible, to express one thing in terms of another thing which it somehow resembles, but from which it is nevertheless diverse throughout." [9] And analogy, he insists, is "only another name for sober and appropriate images." [10]

Like philosophers, poets use images to try to express the mysteries of human existence. Unlike philosophers, they do not continually try to criticize and refine their own images, because in a good poem the images and the pattern they form have an inevitability about them. One cannot ask a great poet to say more or less, or to say it in some other way. One merely says, this is good, this is right. Nor can one ask a reader to explain just what it is that he grasps through the poem. If he tries, the poetry and the apprehension vanish. The words the poet has used have a literal meaning, pointing to whatever it is they point to, but they also evoke echoes of our own existence and permit us to apprehend its meaning and its possibilities in a richer way.[11]

The inspired writers of the Bible stand midway between the poets and the philosophers, Farrer contends. They are not totally free in their choice of images, nor yet continually critical of them; but they communicate through certain dominant images, and these images are, for Farrer, God-given. We talked earlier of revelation through the coalescence of historical events and their interpretation. Farrer speaks of revelation as the interplay of events and images. Christ himself used the archetypal images of the Old Testament—father and son, king and kingdom, servant and master, for example —to convey his own thought. As a rabbi, he taught in parables, and the parables he used were not just original comparisons, freshly drawn from nature. The apostles used the same master-images to interpret the events of Christ's life and death and resurrection, and the events in turn reinterpreted the images. "The events without the images would be no revelation at all, and the images without the events would remain shadows on the clouds." Revelation, again, is the interplay of the two. The images of revelation, like the images of poetry, cannot be decoded. They "must be allowed to signify what they signify of the reality beyond them." [12]

This sounds as if the Christian were condemned endlessly to repeat the faded metaphors of the Bible, with no license for critical thought about them and no chance of reinterpreting them in changing language in a changing culture. It sounds as if we have here a supreme example of the archaist. But this is not the conclusion Farrer draws from his theory of biblical inspiration. He is calling, remember, for a rebirth of images, not for obscurantism. The Old Testament matrix of images is essential to Christian revelation, but this matrix must live again in the mind. If it is to do so, reinterpretation is necessary. "The work of reinterpretation may include much hard and close intellectual effort, there is nothing dreamy or sentimental about it; but it is obvious that the calculative reason alone can do nothing here." [13]

Even with great intellectual effort and with fresh interpretation, can the images be reborn? The Christ-without-myth school thinks they have vanished beyond recall. Farrer and others who share his conviction that the web of biblical images is the irreplaceable pattern of Christian communication, think they can. There has not yet been enough hard, clear thinking to decide the issue, much less to produce a satisfying idea of how it might be accomplished. It is not enough, although it is certainly a beginning, to tell the would-be apologist that he must first teach his culture and himself how to listen to poetry.

Apologetic theologians at work in this direction, however, have already indicated the trinitarian warrant for future study of the function of images. The Creator, they argue, made man in the image of God. This means that his God-given reason includes creative imagination, in the strong sense of that word. His mind is scaled to the world of which he is a part; it provides the pattern-book for his thinking about God. Images are part of the stuff of revelation, they believe, because images are part of the stuff of life. The principle of incarnation, they would continue, means that God makes himself known in history in the limitations of time and place and language. As Richardson put it, "The Divine revelation in history deigns to clothe itself in the common images of the human imagination of all times and places, as once God himself condescended to clothe himself in a robe of human flesh." [14] The Holy Spirit, they would insist thirdly, is at work within men to open ears and to inspire minds to hear and see reality through the poetic language native to Christian faith.

CHAPTER 12

The Human Predicament

After he decides what language to speak, the contemporary theologian must next decide what to start talking about. Which strand in the intricately woven web of Christian ideas should he pick up first? Systematic theologians who try to rethink and re-express the Christian faith as a coherent whole, traditionally have begun with the doctrine of God. Both the Bible and the historic creeds dictate such a starting point: "In the beginning, God created . . ."; "I believe in God, the Father Almighty. . . ." If one is to explain and interpret Christian thought, why not begin here?

WHAT IS MAN?

Most twentieth-century apologists have chosen a different starting place. Man, they say, has always been his own most vexing problem. Let us begin with ourselves. Such a choice is open to obvious criticism. Traditional Christian ideas of man have much to say about human egocentricity, and it is highly possible that contemporary apologetics are merely providing more evidence of this self-centeredness. It is also possible that, in choosing first man's need and then God's action as their framework, apologists are just following a theological trend which started in the early nineteenth century. Since then, exploration of common human experience and of man's so-called religious feelings has customarily taken precedence in theological discussion over ideas about the God to whom these experiences and feelings point. By accepting this approach automatically, one can easily miss the significant difference between the psalmist's question "What is man that thou are mindful of him?" and the isolated question "What is man?" Nevertheless, any theology must include an anthropology. All thinking about God implies a related view of man. We shall participate in our own century. What can be said with reason and relevance today about the Christian view of man?

In our last chapter we posited two criteria for the Christian spokesman today. First, he must speak to his own culture, using the best knowledge which that culture makes available to him. This means today, of course, that the insights of all the behavioral sciences, including psychology and sociology, must be taken into account in a Christian doctrine of man. The Christian who is antiquated in his psychology or superficial in his analysis of human relationships has not taken seriously the task of apologetic theology. Secondly, in his efforts to speak relevantly to his own day, he must neither distort nor impoverish the Christian faith.

The biblical and historical ideas of man which we have already met insist both that man is a creature and that man is a sinner. Genesis 1 introduces the concept that man is made in the image of God; Genesis 2 and 3 introduce, in the mythological language of the Adam story, the equally important concept that man has always fallen into sin. The fifth-century controversy between Augustine and Pelagius rested on these biblical ideas and reaffirmed the seriousness of sin. At the time of the Reformation, theologians everywhere believed that they were rediscovering Augustinian thought. The Lutheran confession was emphatic that baptized Christians are justified and sinful at one and the same time. The much misunderstood Calvinist teaching about total depravity was trying to express the conviction that the whole man, including his mental faculties, is affected by sin. The sixteenth-century statement on original sin still printed in the Book of Common Prayer supports the traditional view unequivocally: Original sin is "the fault and corruption of the Nature of every man . . . whereby man is very far gone from original righteousness, and is of his own nature inclined to evil. . . . And this infection of nature doth remain, yea in them that are regenerated." [1]

Most people stumbling across this statement during a dull sermon would find it either incomprehensible or repugnant. It must be understood afresh, in the light of current knowledge of human nature. It must be expressed anew, in intelligible language. No one has done more toward achieving both these goals than Reinhold Niebuhr. Niebuhr has influenced a whole generation of clerical and lay theologians. Even more notably, he has affected the entire range of American thought. Politicians and economists, psychiatrists and social thinkers acknowledge indebtedness to him. They respect his voice because it speaks directly and profoundly to the crises of our time.

THE HUMAN SITUATION IN CONTEMPORARY TERMS

Niebuhr's thought about man is etched against the background of a great depression and of two world wars. The understanding of sin which became a central theme through his long career of teaching and writing was born in his experience as a young minister in industrial Detroit from 1915 to 1918. But it is never enough to say that Niebuhr's chief contribution to contemporary theology has been the rediscovery of sin. His Detroit years taught him, rather, to have "a high estimate of human stature," together with "a low estimate of human virtue." Nobility and misery together shape his idea of human nature.

His Detroit years also taught him about the complex power structures in which man must function in industrial society. Individual automobile workers, union organizers, and company executives might have been churchgoing Christians, honestly striving to lead sober, righteous, and godly lives; but their earnest Christian perfectionism was totally irrelevant to the violence of strikes or the suffering of the unemployed. Niebuhr's realism in this respect was clear in the title as well as in the contents of his *Moral Man and Immoral Society*, published in 1932.[2]

In *Reflections on the End of an Era*, issued in the following year, he continued his dual indictment of the old naïve liberalism. "The liberal culture of modernity is defective in both religious profundity and political sagacity," he wrote; ". . . it understands neither the heights to which life may rise nor the depths to which it may sink." [3] In his 1935 *Introduction to Christian Ethics*, the easy optimism of contemporary Pelagians was still under attack. However wholeheartedly a man may want to obey the imperatives of the law of love, it is a practical impossibility. This impossibility is the state of sin in which man is caught, the sin of which he must repent. For Niebuhr, repentance is the discovery that one is unable to be truly responsible or truly moral.

An invitation to deliver the historic Gifford lectures at the University of Edinburgh gave Niebuhr the chance to develop his ideas about the Christian doctrine of man more completely and systematically. As he lectured on human nature in the spring of 1939, war clouds were already gathering over Europe. Before he had completed the second series of lectures—on human destiny—in the fall of that year, the storm had broken.[4] In the midst of that storm, and because of it, men could hear Niebuhr's penetrating voice speaking to their own condition.

The analysis of the human situation in the first part of *The Nature and Destiny of Man* includes two fundamental propositions which inform all of Niebuhr's writings. Man is finite. Yet man is free. Exposition of this propositional paradox takes Niebuhr deeply into the history of Christian thought and broadly into contemporary theories of human nature, but the bare bones of his argument consist of these two assertions. Man, he declares in the first place, is "a created and finite existence in both body and spirit." [5] As a creature, he is akin to all other animals. He is a biological organism, with physical needs which cannot be ignored with impunity. He must eat; he must sleep; he must reproduce his kind. He is limited also by time and by space. Much as he might like to, he cannot be in two places at once, nor can he escape the inexorable process of aging, decay, and death. He is a cork on the river of time. Finitude and limitation are basic facts of his existence.

At the same time, man has the capacity to transcend the limits of his own finitude, the capacity for self-determination. He is a free spirit. For Niebuhr, freedom is the more important fact about man. In the imagination of his heart and the flights of his mind, he can get beyond his own time-bound and space-bound condition. He can determine his own future. He can make history. He, and he alone among the creatures, can contemplate his own end. He knows that he is going to die.

MAN'S ANXIETY AND THE ALTERNATIVE OF FAITH

Man's life, as Niebuhr interprets it, is lived at the intersection of finitude and freedom. Man stands at the juncture of nature and spirit. Human existence in this position is fundamentally precarious, fundamentally anxious. "Anxiety is the inevitable concomitant of the paradox of freedom and finiteness in which man is involved." [6] The anxiety of his condition is not itself sin, but it leads to sin. Unable to accept his condition of freedom-in-finitude, he tries to escape anxiety by denying one or the other pole of his existence. He attempts to live a lie.

One alternative open to him is to escape into finitude, to pretend that he is merely a child of nature. He can concentrate on the satisfaction of his physical needs as if they were his total self. He can indulge his senses until he arrives ultimately at stupefaction. He can, in fact, settle not merely for an animal but even for a vegetable existence. It is noteworthy that Niebuhr does not greatly develop this pole of his thinking about sin in the Gifford lectures. In that context, the sins of sensuality are very clearly a secondary consequence of man's rebellion against his true situation. Drunkenness and gluttony, luxurious living and sexual sins are all ambivalent. They are partly the result of pride, of self-love, as well as of sensuality. They betray the self's seeking to escape from itself by throwing itself "into any pursuit which will allow it to forget for a moment the inner tension of an uneasy conscience." [7] The idea is explicit, however, that man tries in various ways to escape from responsibility, to reject his capacity for transcending his limitation. In this perspective, sensuality is first cousin to the sin of sloth, that radical laziness which leads, for example, to superficial thought about the very complex moral and social facts with which man must cope in the responsible use of his freedom.

Man's flight from reality in the opposite direction interests Niebuhr much more. Every man is an escape artist in this direction. Every man pretends that the flight tower reports ceiling unlimited. His practical denial of human finitude is that old enemy, the sin of pride. Pride can and does manifest

itself in every aspect of human existence. Pride of reason produces in man the illusion that, for any problem, he can be
the judge, the jury, and the advocate all in one. Pride of will
expresses itself not only in the many human attempts to exert
power over others, but also in the subtle inversions of power
which seek to control others through weakness. Moral pride
tempts men to embark on futile programs of perfectionism.
It merges easily into spiritual pride, where partial standards
and relative attainments claim divine sanction. Human ambition knows no limit. It must be attributed, Niebuhr
believes,

not merely to the infinite capacities of the human imagination
but to an uneasy recognition of man's finiteness, weakness, and
dependence, which become the more apparent the more we try
to obscure them. . . . Thus man seeks to make himself God because he is betrayed by both his greatness and his weakness; and
there is no level of greatness and power in which the lash of fear
is not at least one strand in the whip of ambition.[8]

Sin is always both individual and collective in Nie-
buhrian thought. Some of his most incisive commentary on
human pride is directed to our political institutions. Na-
tionalism in all its forms—indeed, all our isms—are expressions of collective efforts to escape from finitude. "There is
no conceivable society," he writes, "in which the pride of the
community and the arrogance of the oligarchs must not be
resisted." This analysis extends pointedly to those today who
idolize democracy in their war with communism:

Each generation is tempted to exalt some particular instrument
of justice, which has succeeded in a given instance, as the absolutely essential instrument of justice; or to attribute injustice to
some particular institution or policy which has been the particular cause of particular evil, but is falsely understood if interpreted as the final cause of all social evils. Our best hope of a

tolerable political harmony and of an inner peace rests upon our ability to observe the limits of human freedom, even while we responsibly exploit its creative possibilities.[9]

Thus, for Reinhold Niebuhr, the anxiety integral to human life leads in opposite directions to two different root sins. "When anxiety has conceived it brings forth both pride and sensuality. Man falls into pride, when he seeks to raise his contingent existence to unconditioned significance; he falls into sensuality, when he seeks to escape from his unlimited possibilities of freedom, from the perils and responsibilities of self-determination by immersing himself into a 'mutable good,' by losing himself in some natural vitality." [10]

A third alternative open to man substitutes reality for illusion, but complete realism is an impossible possibility. Man cannot escape from the ambiguities of his existence nor from the anxieties they produce, but he keeps on trying. Although sin is not necessary, as Niebuhr analyzes it, it is inevitable. "Original sin" is the bias toward sin produced by the anxiety in which all life stands; but anxiety alone is neither actual nor original sin. Sin can never be traced merely to the temptation compounded of a situation of finiteness and freedom.[11] It is presupposed in the felt fact of responsibility.

Man is confronted, then, with an ultimate paradox of which the Christian doctrine of original sin is an expression. It makes seemingly contradictory assertions about the inevitability of sin and man's responsibility for that sin. The paradox does justice, Niebuhr believes, to the fact that man's self-love and self-centeredness are inevitable, and yet that precisely in the acknowledgment of that fact man affirms his highest freedom. For "man is most free in the discovery that he is not free." [12]

It is at this point that Christian faith must enter. Christ is, for Niebuhr, the judge of the self-will and the self-righteousness of every individual and of every social group.

The final resistance to pride, he declares, must come from the community which knows and worships a God to whom all men and all nations are subject.[13] The nature of the faith that leads to this worship will be our subject in the next chapter.

That faith itself should be our next topic, is indicated by the surprising correlation between Niebuhr's analysis of the human condition and that of the secular humanist Erich Fromm. In *Man for Himself,* published in 1947, Fromm also undertook to draw a tentative picture of human nature on the basis of empirical sciences such as psychology and anthropology. Like Niebuhr's, his picture is one of a polarity in the human situation. On the one hand, man is the most helpless of animals, biologically weaker even than a robin in the absence of instincts comparable to those which the baby bird inherits. On the other hand, in his self-awareness, his reason, and his imagination whereby he transcends nature, he is the freak of the universe. This polarity, as Fromm sees it, results in some unavoidable disequilibrium in human life, in some insoluble dichotomies.[14]

The only creative way in which man can harmonize the dichotomies of his existence, for Fromm as for Niebuhr, is through his faith. "Man cannot live without faith," he writes. "The crucial question for our own generation and the next ones is whether this faith will be an irrational faith . . . , or the rational faith in man based on the experience of our own productive activity." [15] For Fromm, as we have already had occasion to note of humanists in general, the proper object of faith is man himself—man's capacity for reason, for love, for productive work, for freedom. He must face the truth that he is alone in a universe indifferent to his fate, and put his faith in his own powers. Similar understanding of the human predicament leads both men to the question of faith. It brings into sharp focus not only the question of what one is to have faith in but also what faith is and where one gets it.

Review of Reinhold Niebuhr's thinking about human nature also leaves us with a further question. On the America of the forties, Niebuhr had the impact of a prophet. At every point, he helped men to understand their own times and their own heritage. No other theologian in this century has had such conspicuous success in leading men to rediscover the depths of the Christian understanding of sin, while insisting always on the fact of man's responsible freedom. In both language and content, his thought meets with full marks the dual criteria which we have set for an apologetic theology.

One cannot help wondering, however, whether sin is an adequate starting place for apologetic theology in the sixties. At the time of these Gifford lectures the results of human sin were writ large in daily experience. Man was gazing directly into the abyss of human evil. He did not need to look far for terrifying examples of nationalistic pride. He did not have to dig deep to uncover his own insecurity, his own uneasy conscience. The world situation has certainly not changed so much that it invalidates this analysis of sin. But has it changed enough to make some other word the first word that Christians must speak to their new age? To this question we shall return in thinking about the Church and the world today.

CHAPTER 13

The Nature of Faith

If one asks the casual secularist for a definition of faith, he is apt to get in answer some version of the classic "opiate of the people" theory. If one asks the conventional Christian, he is likely to be told in some way that faith is belief in spite of the evidence. Better-informed Christians, having heard at least indirectly the distinctions which the Reformation brought to man's attention, may define it as trust in spite of the consequences. The problem of faith for contemporary thought is not solved, however, simply by introducing in other words this inherited distinction between *assensus* and *fiducia*. Especially in a world which is increasingly happy to acknowledge that faith-in-general is A Good Thing, relevance demands that one say something more on the subject. Bargain-counter faith can be a dangerous travesty. What more is today's believer to say to distinguish Christian faith?

Two Christian thinkers who have paid particular attention to the nature of faith in modern times can help one get beyond capsule formulae to real thinking on the subject. One is Søren Kierkegaard, the father of modern existentialism. The other is Paul Tillich, perhaps the best-known theologian in America. Although he wrote over a century ago, Kierkegaard's thought is fully as alive as that of Tillich, who regularly makes the cover of *Time* magazine.

KIERKEGAARD'S EXPLORATION OF THE MEANING OF FAITH

Kierkegaard was a theologian who deliberately used the methods and the language of a poet. Almost half of his writings are expressed in what he called indirect discourse, consciously appealing to æsthetic levels of response. Even when he is directly discussing Christianity, his style is that of a literary artist. He chose his oblique approach as part of his revolt against the stereotyped Christianity of his day, with its own pat and pious answers to offer every questioner. Throughout his brief and lonely adult life, ending in 1845, Kierkegaard engaged in attack on Christendom as represented by the Danish State Church. Its leaders symbolized for Kierkegaard the sterility of so-called faith. He was preoccupied always with the question of authentic faith, with the problem of becoming truly a Christian.

Perhaps his deepest exploration into the meaning of faith is found in a short pseudonymous work he published in 1843, *Fear and Trembling*. For Søren Kierkegaard, faith is "a tremendous paradox," which is difficult to understand. To probe the paradox, he therefore invites the reader of *Fear and Trembling* to go with Abraham, "the Father of Faith," on his three days' journey to Mount Moriah to sacrifice his son Isaac. Before reading *Fear and Trembling,* one should reread the Genesis 22 story on which it is based. The Bible does not explore Abraham's state of mind as he traveled across the desert in response to the horrifying command from God to go kill his only son, the one whom he loved, the one whom God had given to him in his old age. With typical economy of expression, the account merely announces that Abraham got up early in the morning, saddled his ass, and started out. Then, "on the third day Abraham lifted up his eyes and saw the place afar off" (22:5).

What would a man think about hour after hour on such an agonizing journey of faith? Bible readers seldom stop to wonder. "It is said to be difficult to understand the philosophy of Hegel; but to understand Abraham, why that is an easy matter!"[1] Kierkegaard makes one face the difficulty as he faced it himself. "Whenever I attempt to think about Abraham," he confesses, "I am, as it were, overwhelmed. At every moment I am aware of the enormous paradox which forms the content of Abraham's life, at every moment I am repulsed, and my thought, notwithstanding its passionate attempts, cannot penetrate into it, cannot forge on the breadth of a hair."[2]

In spite of the difficulties, Kierkegaard did not himself stand paralyzed by the mystery. Here and in other writings, his analysis recognizes four stages of the journey, or four movements in the paradox of faith. One must first recognize the scandal of particularity in this story. Abraham is not a heroic figure, dramatizing generalized truths on a cosmic stage. He is a man asked to kill his own son, whom he loves. It is easy for the reader to equate Isaac with "the best," and then to talk glibly about Abraham's willingness to sacrifice this generalized best-that-he-knows. But this is to side-step the real issue. The demand was in very particular terms. It was not even just to kill "your son," but "your only son Isaac." Isaac was . . . Isaac. Be dismayed, be scandalized at this, Søren Kierkegaard says, or else consign Abraham to oblivion.

To kill Isaac was murder. There is no possibility of understanding Abraham, the knight of faith, if we soften this fact. Here is the second offense to the ethical man. Real faith is outside the category of the ethical. It is "a paradox capable of transforming a murder into a holy act." For this to be the story of faith involves a suspension of the ethical. If it were otherwise, Abraham should be prosecuted for murder.

"It was in the early morning. Abraham arose betimes and embraced Sarah, the bride of his old age. And Sarah kissed Isaac, who had taken the reproach from her—Isaac, her pride, her hope, for all coming generations. Then the twain rode silently along their way. . . ." [3] The real temptation in the Isaac story is to do the ethical thing. For Abraham, the ethical had no higher expression than family life. How could God ask him to destroy it? How could Abraham know that he was not mistaken about the command? How could he draw the knife to kill? Only, Kierkegaard says, by infinite resignation, an agony of infinite resignation. By resigning all finite values. By resigning all finite claims to be in the right. By resigning all conscience, and indeed all consciousness—of intellect, feeling, will—so that there was no question of human calculation any more.

Infinite resignation is, then, a movement of the self, not of thought. It is the last stage Abraham loses sight of before he arrives at faith. It results in the fourth movement, which is a return to the immediate, the finite. Abraham gets Isaac back again. He returns home. His feet are firmly treading the ground of this world. "He smokes his pipe in the evening, and to look at him you would swear it was the greengrocer from across the street who is lounging at the window in the evening twilight." [4] He lives at peace, in the "happy passion" that is faith—a happy passion purchased at the highest price. At every moment, Kierkegaard contends, "He makes not the least movement except by virtue of the absurd . . . this man has performed, and is performing every moment, the movement of infinity. . . . He has resigned everything absolutely and then again seized hold of it all on the strength of the absurd. . . ." [5]

Contemporary existentialists make so much of Kierkegaard's *leap* into the Absurd that it sounds like a one-way

street. It is interesting to note, in *Fear and Trembling,* how
firmly faith is caught between the double movement of infinite resignation (the instant before jumping, as it were) and
the instantaneous return to finite involvement. His knight of
faith "takes pleasure in all things, is interested in everything,
and perseveres in whatever he does with the zest characteristic of persons wholly given to worldly things." [6]

It is crucial to note how constantly he applies the scandal
of particularity to the notion of the Absurd. Abraham notwithstanding, his knight of faith is pre-eminently a Christian
knight. He is interested, we have said, in the problem of
becoming a Christian. Just as in the Abraham story one cannot translate the demand to kill Isaac into some vague idea
of willingness to sacrifice the best, so one cannot digest or
convert the Christian paradox into a general syllogism.[7] The
height of absurdity is specifically the invitation addressed to
all men by Jesus Christ: "Come unto me all ye that travail
and are heavy laden, and I will give you rest."

The person who issues this invitation is, for Kierkegaard,
the same one who issued it 1800 years ago. "It is Jesus Christ
in his lowliness, and in the condition of lowliness. . . . A
believer one cannot become except by having gone to him in
his lowly condition—to him, the rock of offense and the object of faith." [8] If a gentleman clad in a silken gown were
doing the inviting, Kierkegaard says in *Preparation for a
Christian Life,* with a Christmas tree in the background laden
with splendid gifts he intended to distribute, then anyone
would accept. But the low-class person who is actually inviting men to Christian faith is one they can associate with only
at the risk of being ridiculed, of being cast out from respectable society, and perhaps of losing their lives. And when
an invitation involves this, SK observes, it would be human
to say, "No, thank you, in that case I prefer to remain deaf
and blind and lame and leprous." [9]

THE TILLICHIAN PHILOSOPHY OF FAITH

The nineteenth-century Danish theologian wrote in figure and metaphor; his readers must use the glass of vision. Paul Tillich, his twentieth-century companion in the analysis of faith, writes chiefly in the language of the philosopher. He once claimed that he began thinking about infinity at the age of eight. Now in his seventies, he is trying consciously to stand on the border line between philosophy and theology, and to answer the questions which the philosophic mind raises. The description of boundary-line theologian is useful in trying to understand Paul Tillich's thought. He is genuinely an apologetic theologian. To this end, he has one foot in religion and the other in culture; one in the Church and the other in society; one in philosophy and the other in theology. As a result, he can be heard by the intellectual world of today as almost no other Christian thinker of his stature.

In terms of the two approaches we described to the language of faith, Tillich sides with Bultmann, although he is by no means in total agreement with Bultmann's thought. He wishes, as he says in the introduction to his book *Dynamics of Faith,* that we could drop the word *faith* from religious language completely, because it confuses and misleads so many. Since there is as yet no substitute term, however, he proposes to reinterpret the word, hoping to eliminate all the false connotations.

Three distortions of the idea of faith prevail in our day, Tillich believes. They all identify faith with some part of the personality. One such limitation thinks of faith as a type of knowledge, as belief on a low degree of evidence. This is the intellectualistic error denounced four hundred years ago; but Tillich finds it still very much alive in the contemporary scene. A parallel error identifies faith either with determination to believe or with obedience to ethical imperatives. It shuts faith up in the will. And in addition to this voluntaristic view, one encounters also the view that faith is primarily an emotional matter—a subjective feeling, warming the cockles of the heart.

Instead of being the exclusive property of some one part of the psyche, faith, as Tillich explains it, is the central phenomenon of a man's life. He defines faith as "the state of being ultimately concerned." [10] Subjectively considered, it is a centered act of the whole personality. Viewed objectively, it is directed toward that which is ultimate or unconditioned. "One is ultimately concerned," Tillich writes, "only about something to which one essentially belongs and from which one is existentially separated." [11] Thus for Tillich, as for Kierkegaard, the proper correlative of faith is not doubt, but sin; yet in his valiant effort to retool the Christian vocabulary, Tillich wishes to speak, not of original sin, but of "universal estrangement." Ultimate concern is, then, an activity of estranged man directed toward that unconditioned ground of being from which he knows in the depths of his own existence that he is separated.

The history of religions has been dominated by two types of faith, according to Tillich. One type expresses ultimate concern through an idea of the law, an idea of some consecrated order which is to determine the daily lives of people. Confucianism, ethical humanism, Islam, and Talmudic Judaism are all variant expressions of this moral type of faith. In contrast, the ontological type of faith sees the ultimate ground and meaning of reality in a concrete piece of that reality. Any piece of reality has the possibility of becoming a bearer of the holy. Not only the familiar forms of sacramental religion belong to this type, therefore, but also romantic humanism, which sees the divine manifest in man.

In the New Testament experience of faith—"the state of being grasped by the divine Spirit" [12]—Tillich finds a synthesis of moral and ontological types. The divine power is present in man as the spirit of love, justice, and truth. "I would not hesitate to call this . . . the answer to the question and the fulfillment of the dynamics which drive the history of faith," he writes. "But such an answer is not a place to rest upon. It must be given again and again on the basis of new experiences, and under changing conditions." [13]

Hence, for Tillich, one must go on to speak of the life of faith. It is a life demanding courage. It is a life necessitating action. And it is a life which requires a community for its expression, an expression that is always in terms of symbol and myth. Such a living faith is far removed from faith which is a traditional attitude "without tensions, without doubt, and without courage." Tillich does not want totally to dismiss the possibility that this kind of traditional attitude may break through to an actual concern, however. He suggests that while conventional faith is "the dead remnant of former experiences of ultimate concern," the experiences lie dormant in their symbols.[14] Thus even in communicating only the symbols of faith to children, instead of waiting for them to ask their independent questions about ultimate meaning, parents may transmit something which is potentially powerful and living.

Ultimate concern necessarily finds expression in symbol. For the Christian, the central symbol of faith is the cross. Any faith can become idolatrous—by which Tillich means that it can be concerned with what is less than ultimate—and any symbol can become powerless, especially when it is given absolute validity. But Tillich believes that the event which created the chief Christian symbol of the cross provides a protection against the idolatrous element in faith, precisely because it implies an element of self-negation. Every truth of faith and every symbol of faith must stand under judgment by the ultimate; none can put itself in place of the ultimate. The criterion of the cross gives a man courage to affirm his faith in Jesus as the Christ, Tillich says, because "out of this criterion comes the message which is the very heart of Christianity . . . namely, that in spite of all forces of separation between God and man this is overcome from the side of God." [15]

Kierkegaard and Tillich write about faith in different languages, and the differences between them go beyond the merely temperamental, so that it is more than a matter of choosing whether one wants to listen to poetry or prose. The Danish knight of faith, for example, is a lonely rider; he never admits the need of that community through which the Tillichian state of ultimate concern becomes actual. But at two points there is profound agreement between their ideas of the nature of true faith. In part this is because Tillich has been greatly influenced by Kierkegaard, whom he discovered while he was still in graduate school in Germany before the First World War. In greater part it is because they are both speaking as Christians to a world where Christianity has so largely become a merely conventional, and therefore a false, form of faith. Both men agree that faith involves the total self, and both insist that it is by nature a matter of movement from moment to moment.

Neither the mind alone nor the will alone, nor the emotions alone, can leap in behalf of the whole self. Where there is concern for that which is truly ultimate, there is a power integrating the personality. They say it differently, but they say it with equal force. The mature man of faith, for Tillich and for Kierkegaard, is not a religious man; he is a whole person.

When faith is conceived of as dynamic instead of static, furthermore, it means that it can never be something one *has* —as the Boston ladies are said to have their hats, never to buy them. Søren Kierkegaard's Abraham did not come home from Mount Moriah to settle down in possession of faith. He was said to perform every moment the movements of the journey.

Tillich's discussion of the dynamics involved sees an answer which must be given again and again, under ever changing conditions. To think either of the knight of faith or of the courage to be, is to think of new risks every day in a life of constant adventure.

CHAPTER 14

The Church and the World

When Reinhold Niebuhr discussed sin as inevitable in the human condition, he felt compelled to talk about corporate sin, about immoral society. When Paul Tillich talked about the dynamics of faith, he included the community of faith as an integral part of its expression. Both writers share in one of the most significant developments in Christian thought in recent decades—a recovery of the importance of the Church. In some measure this major change in theology merely reflects general intellectual trends. Ecclesiology (or ideas of the Church), group dynamics, and communism have a common backdrop. The twentieth century is aware of the community. In its new preoccupation with the Church, however, Christian theology is also recovering a part of its own heritage.

THE MODERN RELIGIOUS SCENE

Contrary to popular opinion, the Church idea was submerged as a result, not so much of the Protestant Reformation

170

alone, as of a long, complex process toward individualism, intensified in America by the frontier spirit as well as by the separatist temper in Protestant churches. By the early years of this century, interest in the Church had virtually disappeared from religious thought. In 1902 William James could define religion as what a man does with his solitude. Such a definition would be unthinkable today. Now one can scarcely pick up a religious periodical without finding there some discussion of the nature and function of the religious community.

The recovery is not unadulterated gain. Increased thought *about* the Church and increased attendance *at* church are related in people's minds and in social fact. They result in a new form of an old problem for the Christian thinker. With almost everyone in suburbia and scarcely anyone in the inner city going to church, one is forced to ask what the Church really is and how it is related to the world of which it is a part. Many would say, indeed, that thought about this question must have priority over all others which confront the apologist. For nowhere is the irrelevance of the Church more clearly exposed than in the empty caverns of downtown Gothic on weekday mornings—unless it is in the crowded Sunday coffee hours in suburban modern parish houses.

Many powerful prophetic voices are busy denouncing the anomaly of the American religious scene. Like Amos and Hosea in the eighth century B.C., they pronounce God's judgment on our feast days, the noise of our solemn assemblies. They remind us that all human institutions tend to become idolatrous, the institution of religion among them. Like Tertullian in the third century, they demand a separation of Christ from culture, in reaction against the bland Clementine assumption that Christ and the best in our culture are one and the same. With holy vehemence, they repeat Archbishop Temple's conviction that God is not only, or even chiefly, interested in religion.

One of the most cutting, because it is one of the coolest, of such prophetic voices is that of Will Herberg. With the detachment of a sociologist, he examined the three major religious groups in America to discover what functions religion really is serving. He concluded in part that calling oneself a Protestant, Catholic, or Jew provides the uprooted, mobile American with the security of a self-identification label. It does what the old home town did for a man's sense of belonging. In part, church membership testifies to what the jargon would call the other-directed adjustment of peer group conformity. To belong is now the thing to do. And, in part, religion in our country is being used to bolster, virtually to deify, the American way of life. What Herberg means by this becomes appallingly clear when he quotes from an address to the American Legion during its 1955 "Back to God" campaign. The speaker, Dwight D. Eisenhower, declared that "recognition of the Supreme Being is the first, the most basic, expression of Americanism. Without God, there could be no American form of government, nor an American Way of Life." [1]

The contrast between this picture of American religion and the biblical picture of faith is complete. Prophetic faith calls, not for religious conformism, but for maladjustment to one's culture. Peter L. Berger, another of the contemporary prophets, therefore sees the present task of the Church as the task of dis-establishment. "What is required in our situation," he writes, "is a new sense of the freedom of the Church." [2] He does not mean that the Church must become a sort of un-American enclave living on the margins of society, but he does believe that Christian faith requires at least some degree of alienation from the culture. Along with similar critics of conventional Christianity, he concludes his judgment on the religious situation with imperatives—including the imperative for theologians to rethink ecclesiology, the doctrine of the Church, so that it will impinge more nearly on the empirical data of the sociologists. For unless theological thinking is related to genuine social reality, Mr. Berger believes, it becomes mere ideology, mere illusion.[3]

Diagnosticians like Herberg and Berger are welcomed with relief by Christians who find their church meetings uncomfortably indistinguishable from Rotary Club or the A.A.U.W. Yet they have a notable tendency to talk chiefly about what the Church ought to be. The job of the apologetic theologian is to talk about what the Church is—to talk in the indicative, not just the imperative. And the sad fact is that keen sociological prophets greatly outnumber relevant ecclesiologists today, men who can help articulate a positive doctrine of the Church which makes sense within the reality of the suburban captivity of the churches.

Two theologians who do speak with relevance about the Church and the world today are Dietrich Bonhoeffer and Frederick Denison Maurice. Like Tillich and Kierkegaard, they lived a century apart; yet they speak with almost equal sharpness to the situation in the sixties. Unlike Tillich and Kierkegaard, they show no evidence of direct influence of the one on the other; yet there is an amazing congruence in their thought.

THE CHURCH IN THE MIDST OF LIFE

In the last half-dozen years, Dietrich Bonhoeffer's name has become very popular in theological circles, so popular that everyone seems to feel he must put in a plug for Bonhoeffer, just to let his listeners know that he is *au courant*. There is faddism in theological matters, as in everything, and it may well be that some of Bonhoeffer's current vogue is no more than this. Certainly his own dramatic life story and his use of phrases which illuminate our own problems of religiosity help to account for his growing renown. But beyond both his romantic appeal and his keywords for self-understanding, Bonhoeffer offers courageously fresh thinking about Christianity today.

Dietrich Bonhoeffer was a modern Christian martyr. He was one of the first German Christians to be marked as an enemy of the Nazi regime. On February 1, 1933, two days after Hitler was installed as Chancellor of the Third German Reich, Bonhoeffer—then a young theology teacher at the University of Berlin—delivered a radio address pointing out the dangers of idolatry in the Fuehrer concept. Before he could finish, the program was cut off. The authorities recognized already that Bonhoeffer was a dangerous critic.[4]

Shortly thereafter, Bonhoeffer spent two years in London as pastor of German-speaking congregations. Before the Second World War broke out, he accepted an invitation to teach at Union Theological Seminary in New York, where he had earlier done graduate study. But on both occasions he felt impelled to return home to share the trials of his own people. Back in Germany, he directed a small illegal seminary, moved several times to avoid official notice before it was finally disbanded by the Gestapo. Forbidden to speak in public or to publish, he nevertheless continued to write while taking an active part in the political underground. During the war he managed to keep in contact with ecumenical church leaders, and even to make trips to Switzerland and Sweden. Arrested in 1943, he spent two years in prisons, including Buchenwald. Just a few days before the Allies liberated his last prison camp in April, 1945, Bonhoeffer was executed by hanging. He was not yet forty.

Bonhoeffer's seminal ideas about the Christian faith and life were born in the midst of this struggle and persecution. It is hardly surprising that they could not grow fully or be given formal development. One is reminded of Ignatius of Antioch, that second-century Christian whose thinking is known to us through letters he wrote en route to execution in Rome. For Bonhoeffer did not live to complete the syste-

matic *Ethics,* which he considered his major life work, and
the ideas which have so captured the imagination of the contemporary theological world are expressed chiefly in letters
he wrote to a friend from Nazi prison. It is in these prison
letters, necessarily in fragmentary and incomplete form, that
he invites us to explore "a religionless Christianity" in "a
world come of age."

The world come of age, as Bonhoeffer understood it, is
a world which no longer needs religion. It is a world which
no longer needs the idea of "God" as a working hypothesis to
account for the inexplicable or the uncomfortable dimensions
of life. He believed that the movement toward the autonomy
of man, which has been under way since the thirteenth century, has reached a certain completion. "Man has learned to
cope with all questions of importance," he wrote after a year
in prison,

without recourse to "God" as a working hypothesis. In questions
concerning science, art, and even ethics, this has become an understood thing which one scarcely dares to tilt at any more. But for
the last hundred years or so it has been increasingly true of religious questions also: it is becoming evident that everything gets
along without "God," and just as well as before. As in the scientific field, so in human affairs generally, what we call "God" is
being more and more edged out of life. . . .[5]

The trouble with most Christian apologists, Bonhoeffer
thought, is that they want to make a last-ditch stand against
this self-assurance of the modern world, to find some room
left for God and religion on the boundaries of life. The letters
are not always clear as to what he meant by the religious
premise of man; but it includes summoning God to prop up
human weakness, both intellectually and personally. It includes using the words of religion as a substitute for thinking,
as a take-it-or-leave-it answer to questions at the limits of our
perceptive faculties. It includes using the words of religion

as an offer of "cheap grace" on the borders of human existence, where a man can be made to admit inner meaningless-
ness or guilt or despair:

The time when men could be told everything by means of words,
whether theological or simply pious, is over, and so is the time
of the inwardness and conscience, which is to say, the time of
religion as such. We are proceeding towards a time of no religion
at all; men as they are simply cannot be religious any more.[6]

Psychotherapists have been just as guilty as Christian
apologists, Bonhoeffer believed, of a kind of spiritual black-
mail. He was violently opposed to any such boundary-line
approach, whether in secularized or religious form. "Wherever there is health, strength, security, simplicity, they spy
luscious fruit to gnaw at or to lay their pernicious eggs in.
They make it their object first of all to drive men to inward
despair, and then it is all theirs." [7] But this approach can
touch only a small number of people in an adult world,
people who regard themselves as the most important thing in
the world. The ordinary man who spends his everyday life
at work and with his family "has neither time nor inclination
for thinking about his despair and regarding his modest share
of happiness as a trial, a trouble or a disaster." [8]

This man does not need religion, but he does need Christianity. Bonhoeffer did not spell out in any satisfactory form
just what a religionless Christianity would be like. He has
passed that task on to a generation of post-Bonhoeffer theologians who are continuing his attempt to distinguish Christianity from the forms and structures of religion, and to reinterpret Christianity along the lines he suggested. He did
lay down the lines, however. Contrary to the conclusions one
might jump to on hearing the phrase "religionless Christianity," the lines include God, Christ, and the Church. But all in
the midst of life, not on its edges.

God, as Bonhoeffer speaks of him, is the Beyond in the midst of life. We cannot wait until we are at the end of our tether to look for him, Bonhoeffer says; we must find him in the center—in health and vigor and activity, not only in suffering and sin. The ground for this lies in the revelation of God in Christ. Christ is not an answer to our unsolved problems, he was not sent as an object of religion. In Bonhoeffer's strongly biblical theology, Christ is the present Lord of the world. "What is above the world is, in the Gospel, intended to exist for this world—I mean not in the anthropocentric sense of pietistic, ethical theology, but in the Bible sense of creation, and of incarnation, crucifixion, and resurrection of Jesus Christ." [9]

Bonhoeffer spent much of his time in prison studying the Old Testament, and he found nothing in it about saving souls. He believed that the focus of everything in the Bible was the kingdom of God on earth. He believed that as a consequence of the Incarnation, in which Jesus bore our whole human nature, all men *are* "with Christ." [10] He spoke about what now is; he affirmed the lordship of Christ even in a world come of age.

What about the Church in religionless Christianity? The present practices and patterns of religion are not the preconditions of salvation, but the Church remains an indispensable part of Bonhoeffer's thinking about Christianity. It is called forth to belong wholly to the world. His meditations on the Sermon on the Mount in *The Cost of Discipleship* make it evident that the task of the Church is to be what it really is, the body of Christ; and this means to be the community of the crucified. "The Incarnation," he writes, "is the ultimate reason why the service of God cannot be divorced from the service of man." [11] Instead of Pharisaic ostentation, then, or that "modest invisibility" which he indicts as practical conformity to the world, Bonhoeffer summons the Christian community to a costly discipleship of being for the world, of living a new life for others, concerned, as Christ was, with penultimate matters—natural, earthly, human.

In effect, Bonhoeffer calls on the Christian community to go underground, just as part of the church in his own nation did during the Nazi regime. It need not worry about speaking religious words or getting men to wear religious self-identification labels. It can safely remain silent, as Christ did. It need not ferret out men's sins of weakness and summon the strength of God to answer them. In keeping with the paradox of the cross, it needs rather to meet the strength of the world with the weakness of God. Christians are in exactly the opposite position from the religious man in what they expect of God, Bonhoeffer says.

Man's religiosity makes him look in his distress to the power of God in the world; he uses God as a *Deus ex machina*. The Bible however directs him to the powerlessness and suffering of God; only a suffering God can help. To this extent we may say that the process we have described by which the world came of age was an abandonment of a false conception of God, and a clearing of the decks for the God of the Bible, who conquers power and space in the world by his weakness. This must be the starting point for our "worldly" interpretation.[12]

And in the next letter he extends the same idea in relation to the task of the Christian. "Man is challenged to participate in the sufferings of God at the hands of a godless world. He must therefore plunge himself into the life of the world, without attempting to gloss over its ungodliness with a veneer of religion or trying to transfigure it. He must live a worldly life and so participate in the suffering of God." [13] Although he speaks here in the singular, real life as Bonhoeffer understood it is *Life Together,* the title he chose for one of his books of meditations. The social note in his thinking is constant, from his doctoral dissertation on the Communion of Saints through to the last chapter of the outline for a book amplifying the thought in his prison letters—the book he never had a chance to write.

As he projected this last chapter, it would have begun with the fact that "the Church is her true self only when she exists for humanity." [14] By writing such a book, Bonhoeffer hoped to do something for the sake of the Church of the future. That there would be such a Church and such a future was part of Bonhoeffer's underlying faith in the promises of God. In spite of the bombs falling around him as he wrote, he believed that man was free to plunge himself fully into the "polyphony of life," because God "still remains Lord of the earth and still preserves his Church." [15]

THE KINGDOM OF CHRIST IN THIS WORLD

Dietrich Bonhoeffer's *Letters and Papers from Prison* have a tonic effect on the contemporary reader, because they make articulate facts of our time which he has only dimly perceived and rarely dared to say out loud. Bonhoeffer's ideas frequently sound excitingly new, but they also sound startlingly similar to those of Frederick Denison Maurice, an Anglican theologian born just one hundred and one years before him. Maurice was therefore an almost exact contemporary of Søren Kierkegaard. He shared the same concern for the great gap between official nineteenth-century Christendom and the revelation of Jesus Christ. "It is a very great and serious question indeed, whether our patronage of 'Christianity' is not subverting the revelation of Christ," he wrote.[16] But unlike the lonely Dane, who retreated into his aloneness to meet the true Christ, the Englishman went out to meet him in the whole range of human life and thought.

Maurice was convinced that all of life belongs to Christ. This central conviction determined the form and content of his best-known work, *The Kingdom of Christ*, published in 1837 just three years after his ordination. Thoroughly committed to the task of apologetic theology, in method he had much in common with Paul Tillich. Maurice also was a theologian of culture. Influenced strongly by the poet-theologian Samuel Taylor Coleridge, who was still living in London when he began teaching there, Maurice believed that theology should start with the felt needs of man. "No man, I think, will ever be of much use to his generation," he said in the letter to Coleridge's son which forms the preface to the first edition of *The Kingdom of Christ,* "who does not apply himself mainly to the questions which are occupying those who belong to it." [17] The major question of his own generation, as he saw it, was whether there is a universal society for man as man. He set out, in *The Kingdom of Christ,* to give an affirmative answer by uncovering the unity and harmony already existing in life.

In the process he looked at the literature, the philosophy, and the politics, as well as at the religion, of his age. In the romanticism of early nineteenth-century poetry, he found a desire for harmony with nature. In his study of Immanuel Kant, he found "the demand for something catholic." In his reflections on contemporary political thought, he found the search for a bond of fellowship among men. Through sympathetic observation of Unitarianism and Quakerism, with which he was personally acquainted in his own family, he noted the same desire for unity. In each case he concluded that there was a need for a wider platform on which to stand, because the narrow platforms of particular systems, parties, dogmas are not adequate for more than a few individuals to stand upon without quarreling and kicking.

Starting out to discover the real questions which men are asking, where they really live and move and have their being, Frederick Denison Maurice came to the conclusion that "theology is what our age is crying for, even when it thinks it is crying to be rid of theology." [18] For theology, as he understood it, is not a matter of capping the column of man's knowledge with ideas about God, but of digging to discover the substructure. Through such digging, he believed, one discovers a unity, a ground of being, which is an "is" and not an "ought." "The knowledge and life of God," he wrote, is "the ground of all human and earthly knowledge and life." [19]

When Maurice spoke positively of the knowledge and life of God he was speaking about Jesus Christ and his Church. Affirmation of the Incarnation was central to his understanding of all of life, affirmation of the lordship of the risen Christ. It was accomplished fact which dominated his thought, not an idea. A biblical theologian ahead of his time, he recognized that the kingdom of Christ was the main subject of the gospels, an outward kingdom in human society. In their detailed picture of Jesus of Nazareth, the Evangelists said to Maurice that Jesus "certainly died, who as we believed, was the Son of God, and the King of Israel; he actually rose with his body, and came among us who knew him, and spake and ate with us: this is the accomplishment of the union between heaven and earth; it is no longer a word, it is a fact." [20] As Maurice read the New Testament, therefore, men are not to gain a kingdom hereafter; they are in possession of it now. They are "to learn its character" and enter into its privileges.

The Church, for Maurice, is the society, the family of those who are conscious of this fact, this kingdom. The kingdom is a kingdom for all mankind, "a kingdom grounded upon the union which has been established in Christ between God and man." [21] Thus the job of the Church, as he views it, is to proclaim Christ's universal headship of the human race. "The Church exists to tell the world of its true Centre, of the law of mutual sacrifice by which its parts are bound together";[22] and of the state which is our human state, "whether we are conscious of it, whether we are in conformity with it, or no." [23]

This state of unity among men rests on the unity of all things in Christ. Speaking in his characteristic indicative, Maurice insists that there *is* a society for mankind which is constituted and held together in the person of Christ. Baptism is a sign of this fact, of the fact "that the enemy has been vanquished, has been declared to have no right or property in any human creature, in any one corner of the universe." [24] Let us therefore claim our true position, he concludes.

Both Maurice and Bonhoeffer believed that the theology of their day was making a mistake in overemphasizing man's sinfulness. Neither one doubted the fact of sin or evil, but each was more concerned with affirming the good news of what Christ has done. In Bonhoeffer's thought, the emphasis was more on his suffering, in Maurice's more on his triumph; but both men firmly called the Church of Christ out into the world, to be for it and with it. And both believed that religion and religiosity could be a block to discovering this reality of Christ; both underlined the difference between the truth of God and human ideas about that truth.

The theology of a Bonhoeffer or a Maurice gives to Christians the freedom to be themselves, distinct personalities in interrelatedness. It reminds the contemporary apologist that Christ died to save the world, and that he rose again to rule it, but that this fact is a fact, whether one acknowledges it or not. Without nervousness or anxiety, they commend an affirmative way in which Christians can rejoice and be glad in a world which God has made and remade, and in which he stands already in the center of the city as well as on its edges.

CHAPTER 15

Toward an Ecumenical Theology

The many ideas about the Christian faith expressed by many different minds in many different ages are much like the pieces of a giant jigsaw puzzle. The scattered pieces of a puzzle cannot possibly convey the whole picture. Spread out on a card table, they are just an unintelligible mass of shapes and colors. Even when they have finally been assembled, the picture they form is only an approximation of the reality pictured. The flat landscape, bright with autumn leaves, reflected in a duck pond is still a far cry from the three-dimensional scene it represents.

So it is with Christian theology. If, as biblical faith believes, God is a God of truth, then all truth is of a piece. God must have, as it were, the complete picture. If theologians remember Richard Hooker's advice, however, and think they be but men, then they can never expect to put the last piece in the puzzle representing God and man and their relationship. Men and women doing their best to love the Lord their God with all their minds can never arrive at a final answer. Humanly speaking, there is no such thing. But by painstakingly and patiently fitting in the pieces—and rejecting those which are the wrong shape and size—they can work together toward a more coherent whole which bears a trustworthy resemblance to reality.

The analogy has the weakness of all analogies; yet it may suggest that the theological task of the Christian community is necessarily an ecumenical task. In the root sense of that word, it pertains to the whole habitable world. It is universal in scope. In thinking about the task of apologetic theology, of interpreting the faith in ways understandable by the age in which we live, we have been introduced to spokesmen from different parts of the broken Body of Christ. Kierkegaard, Tillich, and Bultmann come out of the Lutheran tradition. Reinhold Niebuhr belongs to the Reformed tradition. Austin Farrer and Frederick Denison Maurice are Anglicans. German, English, American, Danish, they represent different national churches; they write in different languages. Yet each contributes to the common intellectual life of the one, holy, catholic Church of Christ.

THE ECUMENICAL MOVEMENT

The ecumenical movement is perhaps the most important development in the Christian world in the twentieth century. As the word *ecumenical* is now used in Christian thought, it refers specifically to the search for unity in the divided Church, to the movement toward a reunion of separated Christians. Visible achievement of such a united Christendom depends on conscious, dedicated, and difficult effort. No responsible Christian today has any illusion that unity can come on a least-common-denominator basis, ignoring the very real differences in Christian thinking about the truth of God. Ecumenical leaders are committed, rather, to rigorous intellectual labor to deepen understanding both of their own traditions and of those of their separated brethren. Anyone who seeks to promote Christian unity must undertake the same disciplined thinking.

There has always been an ecumenical movement among theologians in the Church. Faced with the scandal of the broken Body of Christ, Christians sometimes think that once upon a time there was an undivided Church. Historical research yields no such golden age in the past. Instead, the evidence indicates that both centrifugal and centripetal forces have been at work in the Christian community from the beginning. New Testament documents testify to tensions and schisms between Jewish Christians and Gentile, for example, from the time of Paul's mission, if not earlier. They record also the attempts of the apostles to reconcile these differences in thought and practice, especially at the so-called Jerusalem Council about A.D. 49, described in Acts 15, when an agreement was reached adapting the faith for those who had not formerly observed the Jewish law.

Different opinions and different practices continued to threaten the unity of the Church, as we have seen. None of the ecumenical councils in the first six centuries was either totally ecumenical, in the sense of representing all of the then Christian world, nor totally successful. The Council of Nicea in 325 ended with the Arians separated from the catholic Christians. The Councils of Constantinople in 381, Ephesus in 431, and Chalcedon in 451 each produced dissident church bodies who called themselves Christians but who were called heretics or schismatics by the majority party. Coptic Christians in Egypt and Ethiopia, to cite just one example, belong to the "Monophysite" churches, which refused to accept the definition of Chalcedon that Jesus Christ was one Person but in two natures, human and divine.

In the familiar words of the hymn, the one Church of

Jesus Christ has always been "by schisms rent asunder, by heresies distressed." The greatest split of all, between Western and Eastern Christendom, occurred in 1054, so that Eastern Orthodox Catholics have been separated from Roman Catholics for virtually a thousand years. But even so, churchmen have been working ever since to heal the Great Schism between the two major groups of Christendom. For all its drama, the Pope's recent visit to the Holy Land, with its attendant irenic moves toward the Orthodox, was only one in a long series of events in the ongoing ministry of reconciliation.

The years of the Protestant Reformation show the same twin forces at work to pull the community of Christians apart and to drive them together. We tend to think of a quick, irrevocable break with the Roman Catholics almost as soon as Luther finished nailing up his theses; but as late as 1684 the Treaty of Westphalia, ending the Thirty Years' War, contained the provisional clause, "until Christendom is reunited." We hear more about the tendency of Protestantism to divide and subdivide into a thousand shattered fragments than we hear about the councils and conferences trying to reconcile their differences; but as early as 1539 the conference at Marburg very nearly achieved theological agreement between Lutheran and Reformed church leaders. Concern for that unity of the Church which Christians daily profess to be a theological fact has never been lost.

Ecumenical enthusiasts today are therefore not the first Christians to take seriously the Lord's charge that they should be one. But they do feel a new sense of urgency about it. The pace of ecumenism has greatly accelerated in our own century, particularly within Protestantism. Some observers of this new ecumenical movement believe that the churches are merely being forced together by cold and whistling winds of the turbulent secular world in which they live. Others believe that obedience is the dominant motive, not self-preservation. There is undoubtedly some truth in both assessments, as well as in the conviction of faith that this new impetus toward unity is God's own action among his people, confirming such biblical declarations as Ephesians 4:4-6:

There is one body and one Spirit, just as you were called to the one hope that belongs to your call, one Lord, one faith, one baptism, one God and Father of us all.

However one analyzes it, the new spirit at work among Christians is already having marked effects on Christian theology.

FORMATION OF THE WORLD COUNCIL OF CHURCHES

The outward events leading to the formation of the World Council of Churches have contributed most to the changed intellectual climate within Protestantism in this century. Three separate branches of the ecumenical movement are now united in the one world body. First came the International Missionary Council, actually started in 1854 but not officially constituted until a world-wide conference at Edinburgh in 1910. This great international organization was the channel for co-operation among the various Protestant denominations in their joint labors to carry the gospel to all parts of the globe.

The second branch grew out of a World Alliance for International Friendship through the Churches, formed in the summer of 1914 and kept going through the First World War, largely by the leadership of Bishop Nathan Soderblom of Sweden. At a Stockholm Conference in 1925 it became the "Life and Work Movement" of the churches, with primary interest, as its title suggests, in Christian social action on the world scene, in economic and political justice. The third such group, the theologically oriented "Faith and Order Movement," was initiated largely because the 1910 Edinburgh meeting of the International Missionary Council quickened the ecumenical vision of an American bishop, Charles Brent. Through his influence, the Episcopal Church in the United States invited churches to come together to study their different ideas of Christian doctrine and church polity. Again the First World War intervened, but the conference finally met in 1927, in Lausanne, Switzerland.

Both the "Life and Work" and the "Faith and Order" movements planned second world meetings in Britain in 1937. Under the guiding hand of such ecumenically minded Christian leaders as William Temple, the two parallel movements voted to merge, combining activism and introspection in "a fellowship of churches which accept Jesus Christ as God and Saviour." A constitutional convention was held in Utrecht in 1938, and the First World Assembly in Amsterdam in 1948, as soon as possible after the Second World War. Since then the World Council of Churches has held two other world assemblies, one at Evanston, Illinois, in 1954, and the last at New Delhi in 1961. At that meeting, the International Missionary Council merged at last with the other two groups.

The New Delhi meeting was also distinguished by the fact that the Russian Orthodox Church then officially joined the world body. The World Council now has 197 member churches in 90 countries, therefore, representing a total of some 300,000,000 Christians. According to the expanded definitive statement adopted at the Indian assembly, it is "a fellowship of churches which confess the Lord Jesus Christ as God and Savior according to the Holy Scriptures and therefore seek to fulfill together their common calling to the glory of one God, Father, Son, and Holy Spirit." In spite of the 15,000-sheet blizzard of mimeographed papers which buried the delegates at New Delhi, the Council is much more than a church bureaucracy, in size and in influence and in spirit. Although it cannot legislate for its member churches, it can and does promote co-operative study and facilitate common action. It maintains permanent headquarters at Geneva,

Switzerland. Increasingly its leadership comes from the younger churches of Asia and Africa.

THE INFLUENCE OF THE VATICAN COUNCIL

Ecumenical has become a common household word in the last few years, however, not primarily through the work of the World Council of Churches, but through the Second Vatican Council. When Pope John XXIII first announced his intention to call such a council in 1959, it was reported that the Pope was about to issue an "invitation to the separated communities to seek for that unity toward which so many hearts in all parts of the world are yearning today." [1] Later official pronouncements clarified the resulting confusion in many minds about the nature of the council. Vatican II, successor of the First Vatican Council of 1869-70, was not to be an ecumenical council of all Christians, but a convocation of the cardinals and bishops of the Roman Catholic Church, aimed primarily at the *aggiornamento,* the updating and renewal, of the Roman Church itself. As one interpreter expressed it, they are trying to correlate a church twenty centuries old with a nuclear age yet to mark its twentieth birthday. Although the *schemata,* or draft proposals, impinging on the doctrine, discipline, and worship of the church which were considered at the first sessions have had wide coverage in the popular press, official results of the Council will not be known until after the final session.

The Vatican Council nevertheless marks a new mood within the Roman Church, a mood favorable to serious discussion with non-Roman Christians. In 1960, in preparation for the Council, the Pope created a special Vatican Secretariat for Promoting Christian Unity, "to enable all those who bear the name Christian but are separated from this Apostolic See . . . to follow the work of the Council and to find more easily the path by which they may arrive at that unity [which

Christ wants]." [2] Under the direction of a German-born biblical scholar, Augustin Cardinal Bea, the Secretariat is an international group and originally included the late Gustave Weigel and George Tavard, theologians already well known to Protestants in America as Roman Catholic leaders in the dialogue which is steadily increasing understanding among the different branches of the holy catholic Church.

RESULTS OF ECUMENICAL DIALOGUE

Dialogue is the word which best describes the present stage of the ecumenical movement on the theological level. Along with a new willingness to listen to one another, there is a new realism about the difficulties involved, and a new readiness to engage in the hard work of making one's own theological ideas understandable as well as of trying really to understand those which are different. Three substantial results of this dialogue are already apparent in the changed theological outlook of the modern world.

Ecumenical dialogue has contributed, first, to a new appreciation of the Bible. Since this book is the common foundation of all Christian thought, the drive toward unity has driven Christians back to the Bible, not for proof-texts to support prejudices—for one can prove anything under the sun, and its opposite as well, in this manner—but for a fresh appraisal of biblical thought as such. Biblical scholarship, as it has developed its own techniques of disciplined research since the late nineteenth century, has in turn contributed to the success of the ecumenical movement in this respect. Relatively objective study, shared by scholars of all faiths, enables Christian thinkers to encounter biblical faith together at primary levels.

An exciting corollary of this biblical rediscovery has been renewed dialogue between Christians and Jews also. It is not accidental that one of the thinkers who exercises a strong influence on contemporary Protestant theology is the Jewish philosopher Martin Buber. Buber is called an existentialist, and rightly so. His profound insights into the nature of genuine encounter between God and man, however, are chiefly the result of his own biblical orientation and his own biblical study. One of the best introductions to Buber's thought is therefore his provocative essay in biblical theology, *The Prophetic Faith*,[3] rather than such a work as his *I and Thou*,[4] whose vocabulary appears so often in Protestant writing. Will Herberg, a Jewish thinker who teaches in a Christian seminary, is another contributor to this dimension of the dialogue. His *Protestant, Catholic, Jew* ends with an incisive summary contrasting American religiosity with biblical faith. It reflects the wide consensus today about what biblical faith really is. Men who stand within the circle of that faith today speak to one another as fellow citizens in the same theological world.

A second and related effect of the ecumenical dialogue is a greater appreciation of the role of tradition in theology, particularly among Protestants. Even as Roman Catholic theologians in the twentieth century are undoubtedly paying more direct attention to the Bible, which Protestants have long accused them of neglecting, so Protestants in turn are alive to a new sense of history, the whole history of the Christian Church. It is no longer possible for a theologian of any denomination to jump over the two thousand years between himself and the primitive Christian community as if nothing significant had happened in the interim. This sense of Christian continuity includes renewed interest in Reformation theology as such, in what is genuinely distinctive in the several traditions of Protestant Christianity. And because the motive has been to get beyond inherited formulae to the reality of the past, various families of Christians have found that some of their differences are imaginary, whereas others are more serious than had previously been imagined.

A third theological result of ecumenical dialogue has been its cumulative, enriching effect on individual Christian doctrines. Each part of the Church has something to contribute, for example, to the idea of the nature of the Church itself—the doctrine which has been so often the focus of thought in the movement designed to reunite it. But more is involved than simply adding up the pieces. Ecumenical biblical study has taught contemporary theologians that in the biblical documents many different metaphors are used to express different ideas about the Christian community. Corresponding study of their respective traditions helps ecumenical theologians to gain perspective about the reasons why one or another of these ideas has been especially favored in their particular communion. The result is not historical relativism, but a new awareness of the many dimensions in the fullness of the idea of the Church.

Christian theology today stands open, then, on two fronts. It is engaged in a dialogue within the Christian family. Each part of the family is contributing to this dialogue. The whole Church is stimulated by it toward creative, fresh thinking about the revelation of God in Jesus Christ. At the same time, Christian theology is engaged in a dialogue with the world of which it is a part. If it is to speak the truth of Christ with relevance to that world, it must speak as a united Church. But it need not speak in a monotone. Even as it calls all men into unity, an ecumenical theology can praise God for diversity.

Notes

Introduction

1. Marjorie Strachey, *The Fathers Without Theology* (New York: Braziller, 1958).

2. Reprinted in *The Pacific Churchman*, May, 1956, p. 20.

Part I. Thinking with the Bible
Chapter 1
Remembered History

1. From Article VI of the Thirty-nine Articles of Religion approved for the Church of England in 1571, *The Book of Common Prayer*, p. 603.

2. Colin M. Turnbull, *The Lonely African* (New York: Simon & Schuster, 1962), p. 214.

3. The illustration, including the quotation from *The Cambridge Modern History*, is drawn from H. Richard Niebuhr, *The Meaning of Revelation* (New York: Macmillan Paperbacks, 1962), p. 60. Mr. Niebuhr's interpretation of revelation has strongly influenced these pages.

4. See esp. G. Ernest Wright, *God Who Acts:* Biblical Theology as Recital (London: S.C.M. Press, 1952); and Wright and Reginald H. Fuller, *The Book of the Acts of God:* Contemporary Scholarship Interprets the Bible (New York: Doubleday Anchor Books, 1960).

5. From the Passover Haggadah as quoted in Arthur Hertzberg (ed.), *Judaism* (New York: Braziller, 1962), p. 127.

Chapter 2
From Exodus to Creation

1. The Five Books of Moses: A new translation of the Holy Scriptures according to the Masoretic Text (Philadelphia: The Jewish Publication Society of America, 1962).

2. "Loving-Kindness," in Alan Richardson (ed.), *A Theological Word Book of the Bible* (New York: Macmillan Paperbacks, 1962), pp. 136-137.

3. For a comparison of the thought in ancient civilizations, see Henri Frankfort *et al., Before Philosophy* (Baltimore: Pelican Books, 1949).

4. A useful introduction to this general field is Theodor Gaster, *Thespis:* Ritual, Myth, and Drama

in the Ancient Near East (New York: Schuman, 1950; Garden City, N. Y.: Doubleday Anchor Books, 1961).

5. See, e.g., G. Ernest Wright and Floyd Filson (eds.), *The Westminster Historical Atlas of the Bible* (rev. ed.; Philadelphia: The Westminster Press, 1956), p. 45, fig. 28. A well-illustrated biblical atlas is an indispensable aid in understanding biblical thought.

Chapter 3
From Resurrection to Incarnation
1. *The Oxford American Prayer Book Commentary* (New York: Oxford University Press, 1950), pp. 168-169.
2. See D. M. Baillie, *God Was in Christ* (New York: Charles Scribner's Sons, 1948), pp. 94ff.
3. C. K. Barrett, *The Gospel According to St. John* (New York: The Macmillan Co., 1955).

Chapter 4
The Expectant Community
1. William Ernest Hocking, "The Freedom to Hope," *Saturday Review* (June 22, 1963), XLVI, 12. Now included in Arthur Larson (ed.), *A Warless World* (New York: McGraw-Hill Book Co., 1963).
2. *Ibid.*
3. For one noteworthy attempt, see H. H. Rowley, *The Relevance of Apocalyptic* (London: Lutterworth Press, 1947).

4. Rudolf Bultmann, *Jesus Christ and Mythology* (New York: Charles Scribner's Sons, 1958), p. 13.
5. *Ibid.*, p. 12.
6. Cf. Oscar Cullmann, *Christ and Time*, trans. F. V. Filson (Philadelphia: The Westminster Press, 1950), p. 145.

Chapter 5
The Response of the People of God
1. Romans 1:24; 4:19; 6:6; 6:12; 7:4; 7:24; 8:10; 8:11; 8:13; 8:23. See Nelson's *Complete Concordance of the Revised Standard Version*, compiled by computer under the supervision of John W. Ellison (New York: Thomas Nelson & Sons, 1957).

Part II. Dialogues with Tradition
Chapter 6
Matter and Spirit
1. *The Meaning of Revelation* (New York: Macmillan Paperbacks, 1962), pp. 141-142.
2. *Of the Laws of Ecclesiastical Polity* (Everyman ed.; New York: E. P. Dutton & Co. Inc., 1954), I, 272.
3. *Ibid.*, p. 268.
4. Peter L. Berger, *The Noise of Solemn Assemblies* (Garden City, N. Y.: Doubleday & Co. Inc., 1961), p. 28.
5. For the Gospel of Thomas, see Robert M. Grant with David Noel Freedman, *The Secret Sayings of Jesus* (London: Fontana

Books, 1960). Robert M. Wilson (ed.), *The Gospel of Philip* (New York: Harper & Row, 1963).

6. Ephesians 7:2. Cyril C. Richardson (ed.), *Early Christian Fathers* ("Library of Christian Classics," Vol. I [Philadelphia: The Westminster Press, 1953]), p. 90.

7. Trallians 9-10, *ibid.*, p. 100.

8. Smyrnaeans 1, *ibid.*, p. 113.

9. Smyrnaeans 6-7, *ibid.*, p. 114.

10. Edward Rochie Hardy, Introduction to Irenaeus in Richardson, *op. cit.*, p. 344.

11. *Against Heresies* i. 13. Cited by Hardy, *ibid.*, p. 346, n. 7.

12. *Again Heresies* iv. 18 ("*The Ante-Nicene Fathers*," Vol. I [Buffalo: The Christian Literature Publishing Co., 1885]), p. 486a.

13. *Against Heresies* v. 33, 36, Richardson, *op. cit.*, p. 396.

14. Justin, *The First Apology* 26, *ibid.*, p. 258.

15. Irenaeus, *Against Heresies* i. 27, *ibid.*, p. 367.

16. *The Apostles' Creed* (New York: Charles Scribner's Sons, 1902), p. 107.

17. Cf. J. N. D. Kelly, *Early Christian Creeds* (London: Longmans, 1950), pp. 65, 144.

18. "The Old Roman Creed," Henry Bettenson (ed.), *Documents of the Christian Church* (New York: Oxford University Press, 1947), p. 34. Italics mine. The Greek word translated *almighty* bears the express meaning of governance of all things.

19. William Temple, *Nature, Man and God* (New York: The Macmillan Co., 1949), p. 478.

Chapter 7
The Deity of Christ

1. Theodore O. Wedel, *Christianity of Main Street* (New York: The Macmillan Co., 1950).

2. Charles Norris Cochrane, *Christianity and Classical Culture* (Galaxy Book ed.; New York: Oxford University Press, 1957), p. 231.

3. Eusebius *Vita* ii. 61 ff; iii. 12 and 21, as quoted by Cochrane, *ibid.*, p. 210.

4. Dorothy L. Sayers, *The Emperor Constantine* (London: Victor Gollanz, 1951), p. 119. Freely adapted from the *Thalia* attributed to Arius.

5. Gregory of Nazianzus *First Theological Oration* 2, Edward Rochie Hardy (ed.), *Christology of the Later Fathers* ("Library of Christian Classics," Vol. III [Philadelphia: Westminster Press, 1954]), p. 129.

6. The Letter of Arius to Eusebius of Nicomedia, *ibid.*, p. 330.

7. Socrates (c. 440) *H.E.* I, v, quoted in Henry Bettenson (ed.), *Documents of the Christian Church* (New York: Oxford University Press, 1947), p. 56.

8. Cochrane, *op. cit.*, p. 249.

9. Sayers, *op. cit.*, p. 116.

10. Summary of the Tome of Constantinople (381), in Hardy, *op. cit.*, p. 343.

11. *Contra Gentes* 28c, as

quoted by Cochrane, *op. cit.*, p. 364.

12. *De Decretis* 11, *ibid.*, p. 365.

13. *On the Incarnation* 4, Hardy, *op. cit.*, p. 59.

14. *On the Incarnation* 1, *ibid.*, p. 56.

15. *On the Incarnation* 9, *ibid.*, p. 63.

16. *On the Incarnation* 54, *ibid.*, p. 107.

17. Hardy, *ibid.*, p. 107, n. 79.

Chapter 8
The Seriousness of Sin

1. *Eichmann in Jerusalem* (New York: The Viking Press, 1963), p. 111.

2. *Ibid.*, p. 253.

3. *Ibid.*, p. 254.

4. See Erich Fromm, *Man for Himself* (New York: Rinehart & Co., 1947).

5. From the Collect for the 2nd Sunday in Lent, which appears first in the 6th-century Gregorian Sacramentary; for the 1st Sunday after Trinity, which appears first in the 5th-century Gelasian Sacramentary; and for Septuagesima, which appears in almost identical form in both ancient Sacramentaries; Massey Shepherd, *The Oxford American Prayer Book Commentary* (New York: Oxford University Press, 1950), pp. 168-169.

6. *Ep.* lx, as quoted by Christopher Dawson, "St. Augustine and His Age," in *Saint Augustine* (New York: Meridian Books, 1957), pp. 37-38.

7. *Confessions* viii. 27, quoted from E. B. Pusey (tr.), *The Confessions of St. Augustine* (Everyman ed., New York: E. P. Dutton & Co., 1945), p. 170.

8. *Confessions* viii. 29, *ibid.*, p. 171.

9. *Confessions* ix, 14, *ibid.*, p. 186; cf. ix. 12, p. 184.

10. *The Enchiridion on Faith, Hope, and Love* xiii, quoted from Henry Paolucci (tr.), (Gateway Paperback ed.; Chicago: Henry Regnery Co., 1961), p. 14.

11. *Enchiridion* xi, *ibid.*, p. 11.

12. *On Nature and Grace* iii, quoted from Roger Hazelton (ed.), *Selected Writings of Saint Augustine* (New York: Meridian Books, 1962), p. 195.

13. *The Spirit and the Letter* 5, quoted from John Burnaby (ed.), *Augustine: Later Works* ("Library of Christian Classics," Vol. VIII [Philadelphia: The Westminster Press, 1955]), p. 197.

14. *The Spirit and the Letter* 11, *ibid.*, p. 201.

15. *The Spirit and the Letter* 17, *ibid.*, p. 207.

16. *The Spirit and the Letter* 18, *ibid.*, p. 208.

17. *The Spirit and the Letter*, 37, *ibid.*, p. 222.

18. *On Original Sin* 17, quoted from Whitney J. Oates, *The Basic Writings of St. Augustine* (New York: Random House, 1948), I, 631.

19. *Enchiridion* i, Paolucci, *op. cit.,* p. 2.

20. *On the Merits and Forgiveness of Sins* i. 19, in Philip Schaff (ed.), *Nicene and Post-Nicene Fathers* (Buffalo: The Christian Literature Co., 1887), Vol. V. Cf. Paul Lehmann, "The Anti-Pelagian Writings," in Roy W. Battenhouse (ed.), *A Companion to the Study of St. Augustine* (New York: Oxford University Press, 1955), p. 215.

21. *Letter 217;* Hazelton, *op. cit.,* p. 216.

22. *Enchiridion* cxviii, cxxi; Paolucci, *op. cit.,* p. 139.

23. *The City of God* xix, 24, quoted from Marcus Dods (tr.), (New York: The Modern Library, 1950), p. 706.

24. *The City of God* xiv, 28, *ibid.,* p. 477.

Chapter 9
Reason and Revelation

1. W. T. Stace, "Man Against Darkness," *Atlantic,* September, 1948, p. 55.

2. Robert McAfee Brown, *The Spirit of Protestantism* (New York: Oxford University Press, 1961), ch. 14.

3. This and the following paragraph are dependent on Etienne Gilson, *Reason and Revelation in the Middle Ages* (New York: Charles Scribner's Sons, 1948), ch. 2.

4. *Ibid.,* p. 6.

5. Etienne Gilson, *History of Christian Philosophy in the Middle Ages* (New York: Random House, 1955), p. 164.

6. Helen Waddell, *Peter Abelard* (New York: The Viking Press; Compass Books ed., 1959), p. 38.

7. Bruno Scott James (tr.), *The Letters of St. Bernard of Clairvaux* (Chicago: Henry Regnery Co., 1953), p. 321.

8. *Ibid.,* p. 328.

9. *Ibid.,* p. 318.

10. *Ibid.,* p. 316.

11. As quoted by James, *ibid.,* p. 316, n. 4.

12. As quoted by James, *ibid.,* p. 314.

13. Waddell, *op. cit.,* p. 6.

14. Gilson, *Reason and Revelation,* p. 73.

15. Herbert Goldstein, President, Association of Orthodox Jewish Scientists, in "Letters to the Editor," *Saturday Review,* May 4, 1963, p. 21.

16. Gilson, *Reason and Revelation,* p. 83.

17. *Ibid.,* p. 84.

18. Anton C. Pegis (tr.), *Summa Contra Gentiles* (New York: Image Books, 1955), Vols. I-IV.

19. *Ibid.,* Book I, Ch. 4.

20. Karl Barth, *Anselm: Fides Quaerens Intellectum* (New York: Meridian Books, 1962), p. 11.

21. *Ibid.,* p. 18.

Chapter 10
Faith and Works

1. "Commentary on Galatians," *Martin Luther*: Selections from his

Writings, ed. John Dillenberger (Garden City, N. Y.: Doubleday Anchor, 1961), p. 130.

2. "The Babylonian Captivity of the Church," *Three Treatises* (Philadelphia: The Muhlenberg Press, 1943), p. 170.

3. *Ibid.*, p. 168.

4. Dillenberger, *op. cit.*, p. 19.

5. *Ibid.*, p. 71.

6. *Ibid.*, p. 55.

7. *Ibid.*, p. 27.

8. *Ibid.*, p. 24.

9. *Works of Cranmer,* edited for the Parker Society by John Edmund Cox (Cambridge: University Press, 1844), I, p. 425.

10. *Ibid.*, p. 130.

11. Article XI, *The Book of Common Prayer,* p. 605.

12. Dillenberger, *op. cit.*, p. 24.

13. Cf. Article XIII, *The Book of Common Prayer,* p. 605.

14. Canons on Justification (Session VI; January, 1547), quoted in Henry Bettenson, *Documents of the Christian Church* (New York: Oxford University Press, 1947), p. 369.

15. John Jewel, *An Apology of the Church of England,* ed. J. E. Booty (Ithaca: Cornell University Press, published for the Folger Shakespeare Library, 1963), p. 138.

16. *Ibid.*, p. 39.

17. *The Works of that Learned and Judicious Divine Mr. Richard Hooker*: with an account of his life and death by Isaac Walton (Oxford: Clarendon Press, 1875), I, 41.

18. *Ibid.*, included in *Of the Laws of Ecclesiastical Polity* (Everyman ed.; New York: E. P. Dutton & Co., Inc., 1954), I, 59.

19. *Ibid.*, p. 75.

20. *Ibid.*, p. 59.

21. *Ibid.*, p. 16.

22. *Ibid.*, p. 37.

23. *Ibid.*, p. 24.

24. *Ibid.*, p. 67.

25. *Ibid.*, p. 45.

Part III. Reason and Relevance
Chapter 11
The Language of Faith

1. *Of the Laws of Ecclesiastical Polity* (Everyman ed.; New York: E. P. Dutton, 1954), I, 121.

2. Alan Richardson, *Christian Apologetics* (New York: Harper & Brothers, 1947), p. 19.

3. Adolf Harnack, *What is Christianity?* (New York: Harper Torchbook ed., 1957). Introduction by Rudolf Bultmann.

4. Amos N. Wilder, *New Testament Faith for Today* (London: S.C.M. Press, 1956), p. 43.

5. Karl Jaspers and Rudolf Bultmann, *Myth and Christianity*: An Inquiry into the Possibility of Religion without Myth (New York: The Noonday Press, 1958), p. 59.

6. *Ibid.*, pp. 67, 69.

7. *Ibid.*, p. 69.

8. See Wilder, *op. cit.*, esp. ch. II; and Alan Richardson, *The Bible in the Age of Science* (Philadelphia: The Westminster Press, 1961), ch. 5. Cf. Schubert M. Og-

den, *Christ Without Myth* (London: Collins, 1962).

9. Austin Farrer, *The Glass of Vision* (London: Dacre Press, 1958), p. 75.

10. *Ibid.,* p. 71.

11. *Ibid.,* p. 121.

12. *Ibid.,* p. 148.

13. Austin Farrer, *A Rebirth of Images* (London: Dacre Press, 1949), p. 17.

14. Richardson, *op. cit.,* ch. 7, "The Theology of Images," p. 158.

Chapter 12
The Human Predicament

1. Article IX, p. 604.

2. New York: Charles Scribner's Sons, 1932.

3. Quoted in John Dillenberger and Claude Welch, *Protestant Christianity*: Interpreted Through Its Development (New York: Charles Scribner's Sons, 1954), p. 259.

4. Reinhold Niebuhr, *The Nature and Destiny of Man* (New York: Charles Scribner's Sons, 1943), Vol. I, p. viii.

5. *Ibid.,* p. 12.

6. *Ibid.,* p. 182.

7. *Ibid.,* p. 234.

8. *Ibid.,* p. 194.

9. *The Structure of Nations and Empires,* as quoted in Harold Landon (ed.), *Reinhold Niebuhr: A Prophetic Voice in Our Time* (Greenwich, Conn.: The Seabury Press, 1962), p. 16.

10. *The Nature and Destiny of Man,* I, 186.

11. *Ibid.,* p. 254.

12. *Ibid.,* p. 260.

13. Landon, *op. cit.,* p. 19.

14. Erich Fromm, *Man for Himself* (New York: Rinehart & Co., 1947), ch. 3, "Human Nature and Character."

15. *Ibid.,* p. 210.

Chapter 13
The Nature of Faith

1. Lee M. Hollander, *Selections from the Writings of Kierkegaard* (Revised ed.; Garden City, N. Y.: Doubleday Anchor Books, 1960), p. 139.

2. *Ibid.*

3. *Ibid.,* p. 123.

4. *Ibid.,* p. 146.

5. *Ibid.*

6. *Ibid.,* p. 144.

7. From *Preparation for a Christian Life*; Hollander, *op. cit.,* p. 174.

8. *Ibid.,* p. 167.

9. *Ibid.,* p. 182.

10. Paul Tillich, *Dynamics of Faith* (New York: Harper & Brothers, 1957), p. 1.

11. *Ibid.,* p. 112.

12. *Ibid.,* p. 71.

13. *Ibid.*

14. *Ibid.,* p. 102.

15. *Ibid.,* p. 104.

Chapter 14
The Church and the World

1. Will Herberg, *Protestant-*

Catholic-Jew (Revised ed.; Garden City, N. Y.: Doubleday Anchor Books, 1960), p. 258.

2. Peter L. Berger, *The Noise of Solemn Assemblies* (Garden City, N. Y.: Doubleday Anchor Books, 1961), p. 138.

3. *Ibid.*, p. 161.

4. John D. Godsey, *The Theology of Dietrich Bonhoeffer* (Philadelphia: The Westminster Press, 1960), ch. 2.

5. Dietrich Bonhoeffer, *Letters and Papers from Prison*, ed. Eberhard Bethge (New York: Macmillan Paperbacks, 1962), p. 195.

6. *Ibid.*, p. 162.

7. *Ibid.*, p. 196.

8. *Ibid.*

9. *Ibid.*, p. 168.

10. Dietrich Bonhoeffer, *The Cost of Discipleship* (New York: The Macmillan Co., 1955), p. 183.

11. *Ibid.*, p. 112.

12. *Letters and Papers from Prison*, p. 220.

13. *Ibid.*, p. 222.

14. *Ibid.*, p. 239.

15. *Ibid.*, p. 242.

16. *What is Revelation?* (1859), as quoted by Arthur Michael Ramsey, *F. D. Maurice and the Conflicts of Modern Theology* (Cambridge: University Press, 1951), p. 42, n. 2.

17. Alec R. Vidler (ed.), *The Kingdom of Christ* (London: S.C.M. Press, 1958), Appendix to Vol. II, p. 359.

18. *The Life of Frederick Denison Maurice,* chiefly told in his own Letters, edited by his son Frederick Maurice (3rd edition, 1884), II, 493. See also, John F. Porter (ed.) and William J. Wolf (ed.), *Toward the Recovery of Unity: The Thought of Frederick Denison Maurice* (New York: Seabury Press, 1964), p. 220.

19. *Ibid.*, I, 59.

20. *The Kingdom of Christ*, I, 251.

21. *Ibid.*, p. 266.

22. *Lincoln's Inn Sermons* I, 251, as quoted by Alec R. Vidler, *Witness to the Light* (New York: Charles Scribner's Sons, 1948), p. 62.

23. *Kingdom of Christ*, I, 272.

24. *Ibid.*, p. 280.

Chapter 15

Toward an Ecumenical Theology

1. See "The Ecumenical Century," *Time*, December 8, 1961, pp. 76-80.

2. Thomas F. Stransky, C.S.P., "Promoting Christian Unity," *America*, March 4, 1961, p. 733. See also George H. Tavard, *Two Centuries of Ecumenism* (New York: Mentor-Omega Books, 1962).

3. Martin Buber, *The Prophetic Faith* (New York: Harper Torchbooks, 1949).

4. Martin Buber, *I and Thou* (New York: Charles Scribner's Sons, 1958).

Index